OAK LAWN PUBLIC
P9-CEM-390
3 1186 00746 7129

"Child problems need parent solutions. That is exactly what Brenda Nixon helps you create for your child. Her easy-to-read style calms you as you learn to guide and support your child."

Sally Goldberg, PhD,
early childhood author, educator, speaker, coach

"Brenda Nixon's new book is not a 'look at everything you're doing wrong' instructional guide for parents. Rather, it is an encouraging and helpful aid to get you through those challenging early years. She answers your questions, treats Mom and Dad as important partners in the parenting process, and she does it all with the spirit of a teacher and coach. I highly recommend Brenda's book to all new parents."

Martha Bolton, Emmy-nominated writer
and author of over fifty books

"Brenda's practical and wise advice will give great peace and knowledge to every parent—regardless of what kind of unpleasant behavior your child is exhibiting. I love Brenda's positive, comforting, and encouraging style. Every parent who reads this book will feel more confident about being a parent. I highly recommend *The Birth to Five Book*."

Kathy Collard Miller,
speaker, author

"Brenda Nixon cuts to the core of exactly what parents need to know in a balanced way that is rooted in wisdom. I can't say enough about her concepts and expertise! Any parents reading *The Birth to Five Book* will find the exact answers they need to meet the challenge of raising children. I wish every parent would read Brenda's books!"

Debra White Smith,
author, speaker, mom

the birth to five book

Confident Childrearing Right from the Start

Brenda Nixon

Revell
a division of Baker Publishing Group
Grand Rapids, Michigan

Published by Revell
a division of Baker Publishing Group
P.O. Box 6287, Grand Rapids, MI 49516-6287
www.revellbooks.com

Printed in the United States of America

Library of Congress Cataloging-in-Publication Data
Nixon, Brenda, 1954–
The birth to five book : confident childrearing right from the start / Brenda Nixon.
p. cm.
Includes bibliographical references.
ISBN 978-0-8007-3319-3 (pbk.)
1. Parenting. 2. Child rearing. 3. Child development. I. Title.
HQ755.8.N587 2009
649′.1—dc22 2008029471

In keeping with biblical principles of creation stewardship, Baker Publishing Group advocates the responsible use of our natural resources. As a member of the Green Press Initiative, our company uses recycled paper when possible. The text paper of this book is comprised of 30% post-consumer waste.

To Lynsey and Laura,
this book's
raison d'être

contents

2. Parenting Your Toddler

3. Parenting Your Preschooler

author's note

This book is intended to inform and inspire you in raising a child and is not a substitute for seeking advice from professionals who know you and your child personally.

acknowledgments

No person is an island. However, when sitting alone in my office, writing for hours on end, I often felt isolated. This book could not have been born without the faithful assistance, advice, and cooperation of many people.

Thank you to the thousands of parents in my audiences who gave me ideas and feedback for this book. I gratefully appreciate those who read portions of the manuscript and offered valuable input.

Thank you, Paul, my terrific husband and best friend, for your confidence in me and for lightening the load of managing our home while I was absorbed in my writing.

introduction

Building healthy, happy families one parent at a time is my passion—my profession—my goal. I am a speaker and writer devoted to parent empowerment through education and encouragement. In 1998, when I was establishing myself on the speaking circuit, the editor of a fledgling kids' publication asked me to write a regular column. That was my birth into the writing world. Although the magazine died three years later, my love for writing grew. Later, a new publication invited me to be its columnist helping parents understand their children and respond with more competence and confidence. With experience, I gained confidence in my writing ability and contributed to various print and online publications.

Often I took my articles along on speaking engagements to give to audiences. Over the years, thousands of parents asked, "Why don't you put your columns into a book?" In 2001, I gathered the favorites and wrote new pieces for my first book, *Parenting Power in the Early Years*. It sold out, and we revised and improved it to become this book.

As in writing, only knowledge and experience in parenting will breed confidence in childrearing abilities. Martin Luther King, Jr., said, “You don’t have to have a college degree . . . You don’t have to make your subject and verb agree . . . You only need a heart full of grace . . . A soul generated by love.” I sincerely hope my words contribute to your knowledge and experience during these foundational years of parenting so you’ll enjoy a healthy, happy family.

In the end, your child will sense your love when you fully embrace this sacred and enormous task.

1 parenting your infant

2

3

4

the right start

"If I only knew then what I know now." I've groaned that sentiment about pregnancy and parenthood many times. When I was expecting my first child, Lynsey, I read parenting books, magazines, and articles to help me prepare. That increased my knowledge and relieved some self-doubts, but there were things I had to experience to learn. Here are nine nuggets I learned early in parenting that I'll share to empower you right from the start.

1. Pregnancy creates a roller coaster of feelings. The highs and lows are linked to the hormonal adjustments of gestation. Plus, the emotional energy it takes to prepare for a new and uncertain phase of life complicates already mixed feelings. This is normal. It's better to share your indecision, wishes, dreams, and doubts than to deny or hold them in.

2. The goal is a healthy baby, no matter how he's delivered. It is wise to take childbirth classes and rehearse the birth; however, plans may go awry. Even women who have given birth before cannot predict how subsequent deliveries will go. Keep labor and delivery expectations realistic and flexible so you don't begin this new path burdened with disappointment.

3. A newborn requires milk, a feeling of being loved, a safe place to sleep, and frequent diaper changes. If you provide these basic four, you're a good enough parent. Don't beat yourself up, buy all the cute nursery decorations, clothes, and toys, or feel anxious to buy everything at once. There'll be enough guilt when you're fully into parenthood. Mother of four and author of *Rattled: Surviving Your Baby's First Year Without Losing Your Cool,* Trish Berg, wisely observes, "My advice is not to waste time with *Baby Einstein* videos. There's nothing wrong with them, but what your baby needs most is *you*. Just you. It really is that simple."[1]

> A child enters your home and makes so much noise for twenty years you can hardly stand it—
> then departs, leaving the house so silent you think you will go mad.
>
> Dr. J. A. Holmes

4. You can't spoil a newborn. It's impossible. His brain hasn't developed to the point of knowing how to manipulate adults. When he cries, it is literally a cry for help. Respond consistently and predictably to his needs. Hold, cuddle, massage, and rock your baby as much as you want because a crucial component for healthy brain development is touch.

5. Don't imagine the worst. A newborn's only concern is relief from discomfort. If he's not crying, he's probably satisfied and content. My husband and I obsessed with our first child. We constantly checked on her to insure that she was breathing and was clean, that the sunlight wasn't in her face, and that the neighbor's dog wasn't barking too loudly. Moreover, we were nervous that she might be crying and we couldn't hear her. And when she wailed in those early days, I didn't always know what she needed. I guessed and did my best; sometimes I was right and sometimes not. It usually takes about six weeks before you accurately "read" your baby's cries.

6. There's no one right way to parent. I loved being a mom, and it was a large part of my identity. I often compared myself to other parents and wanted to do everything right. However, all babies are different, and what worked for a friend or relative did not work in my home. I soon realized that Lynsey and I were going through this adventure together for the first time. She had no frame of reference so she didn't know if my parenting was right or wrong. Parenting isn't a mold in which you pour yourself. Custom design your own style; your baby will adjust.

7. Occasional anger and frustration with a baby is normal. Today there are books on this topic, but when I was a new mom there were few books and no person who told me there'd be days when I wouldn't feel loving toward my daughter. At frazzled times when I was close to my "cool mom" limit, I'd wish I could put her back. I envisioned drop-kicking her out the front door. Then I would be shocked at and feel guilty for those "horrible" emotions. One mom recently emailed me that she sometimes wishes her sons would hurry and grow up. She said there are days when it's just too wearisome being a parent. It is healthier to express those common, human emotions to another adult than to explode into action. When you find yourself feeling angry or frustrated, don't make your baby the target. Instead, acknowledge your feelings, put him down, and talk to another adult. If no one is around, put your baby down and take a "time out"—and remember, a bad day is temporary. Trish Berg suggests taking ten deep breaths, exhaling slowly each time; getting more rest; and saying positive things to others about your baby.[2]

8. There are no perfect parents. So much of parenting is trial and error, guessing, working on instinct, doing the best at the moment. It's easy to feel intimidated and overwhelmed

with the barrage of advice—solicited and not—and with the parenting pendulum that swings from one extreme to the other. One mom confessed, "I feel so stupid," when she didn't know what to do. We don't have to be perfect to be successful. I now know that minor misjudgments or mistakes in parenting—or those bad days—did not scar either of my daughters or ruin their development. It's the long haul of good parenting that counts.

9. Though mothering began at the dawn of human history, the job isn't completely instinctual. Many times my girls have heard me utter, "I've never been a parent before. I'm doing the best I know." You are not expected to be experienced, even if this is your third or fourth child. Each child's temperament is different, as will be your parent/child relationship. You will become better with practice and when you are open to learning how to improve. Just as you would with any career, educate yourself, commit to the job, talk to those who are experienced, and accept support.

I can't go back to those early days, but you are there now. Use these lessons and you'll know right from the start what took me years to learn.

My Success Strategy

Which of these nuggets do I need to remember this week—perhaps repeat to myself—so I'm more confident as a parent?

"is she normal?"

"Is she healthy? Is she normal?" I asked, still lying on the delivery table after the birth of Lynsey. Eye color, who she looked like, or amount of hair didn't matter until I was reassured my baby was in good shape. Those same concerns resurfaced at the pediatrician's office on each follow-up visit. It's natural for parents to have many questions.

Are you anticipating the birth of your baby or have you just entered the door of parenthood? Getting acquainted with your newest family member will be more enjoyable if you are aware of what is "healthy" and "normal." Here are some typical characteristics of infant development.

All newborns are nearsighted. They can see people and objects clearly at a distance of only eight to ten inches. Beyond that, their world looks blurred. Vision is the slowest sense to develop. When you hold your baby in the crook of your arm, he is at the correct distance to clearly focus on your face. Infants love to quietly study your eyes, your forehead, your hairline. Of particular interest is the color contrast between your skin and hair.

Their eyes cross occasionally. "Oh no, Lynsey's cross-eyed!" I shrieked to my husband. Those first six weeks scared me because I wasn't told a baby's inexperienced eye muscles can cause the eyeballs to go all over the place. I've since learned that if this occurs constantly or persists after a baby's sixth week, you should talk with a pediatrician.

> Every child born into the world is a new thought of God, an ever-fresh and radiant possibility.
>
> Kate Douglas Wiggin

Hiccups are common. Because the infant's diaphragm is still maturing, it easily gets out of rhythm. Hiccups can be loud and annoying, but they are not a cause for real concern. By the time my second daughter, Laura, joined us I was more aware of normal hiccups and didn't worry about hers. Boy, did she have them—inside and outside of me. One time at church, we were sitting in the second pew with Laura, and she had hiccups so loud the choir members looked at us and giggled.

Infants startle easily. In fact, the startle reflex is one thing doctors check for immediately after delivery. Any sudden noise, like a loud clap or outburst of laughter, may cause your baby to jolt, flail her arms, or recoil. It looks worse than it is. After the second month this mysterious, harmless reflex disappears.

They don't always burp. Especially if breast-fed, your baby may not have to burp a burp after meals. Less air is taken in at the breast than the bottle. Since I nursed, I wish I had known that as I sat up in the wee hours of the morning patiently, sleepily patting Lynsey. I now know that burping isn't always necessary, but holding a baby is.

Early weight loss is normal. In the first days, most babies lose weight because they excrete excess body waste and don't replace it by eating. Appetite usually comes on the third day. Laura weighed just over six pounds at delivery. When I brought her home, she weighed in at five pounds. I called her my little bag of sugar. Your baby should quickly regain her lost weight. Then, birth weight usually doubles within three to five months.

Spit-up is a common problem. Forty percent of healthy infants regurgitate more than once a day.[1] Because her tiny tummy and digestive system are immature, overeating creates immediate overflow. If your baby is content and gaining weight, she's fine. Spitting up peaks around four months and usually resolves itself by the first birthday when the tummy is larger and mature. Smaller feedings help to correct the mess. Also, that old wives' tale about not jostling the baby after eating is true—it will cut down on spit-up. However, if your baby throws up everything for days or has excessive crying, choking, wheezing, coughing, hoarseness, or projectile vomit, consult your pediatrician.

Crying is communication. It tells you that your baby has legitimate needs; she's hungry, frightened, or uncomfortable. She needs you to respond immediately and consistently to her cries for help. In these first months, it's critical your infant begins to trust you, to learn that you will soothe and attend to her needs. Studies reveal that babies with secure emotional bonds to their parents tend to become more cooperative preschoolers and kindergartners. Now that's a good argument when someone stops you from picking her up with, "You'll spoil that kid!"

Smiling is not real. "She smiled at me!" insists a proud grandma. In the first weeks a newborn does not smile—on purpose, that is. What you see is either muscle reflex or gas relief. Take heart, though; most infants will eagerly gaze into your eyes and give you broad, toothless grins at around five to six weeks of age.

Evening fussiness is common. What if you've done everything right and your baby still cries? The answer may lie in her fragile neurological system. What doctors call "sensory overload" simply means the newborn has become overstimulated with noise, commotion, or people. When this happens, she becomes especially fussy and hard to console. Crying is a way of equalizing her neurological system.

For my girls the restless crying occurred many evenings between 5:00 and 7:00 p.m. It was as if the daily activities built up and overwhelmed them. Sometimes I realized the extra company or errands put them over the edge. To save your ears and your baby's frustration level, try to prevent constant activity in her first months. It's also helpful to plan some quiet time each day.

Newborns are vulnerable. Pound for pound, infants breathe in two to three times more air than adults do. That is why they're more susceptible to the dangers of airborne lead, secondhand smoke, and toxic fumes from new furnishings. Research shows that secondary smoke exposure could cause frequent viral and bacterial infections, including painful ear infections. There is also some research to suggest that smoke may increase the risk of sudden infant death syndrome. For all these reasons, ask adults who smoke to do so outside and away from your helpless baby. Better yet, state, "No smoking."

Even though I wasn't sure what was "normal," I prized those early months of parenting. I indulged in holding, cuddling, rocking, and kissing soft cheeks. I hope you do too.

My Success Strategy

Knowing about infant development helps me feel more competent. I can support my baby's development by . . .

great expectations

There in my arms squirmed a petite, pink baby girl. Eyes squeezed closed, flawless skin, sudden, jerky movements, perfectly shaped lips, and a wondrous button nose. It hit me: I was no longer just a daughter; now I had a daughter. As I clutched this new life, my heart ached under the load of countless feelings. Little did I know I was teetering on the brink of the "uncertainty" pit.

Naively I expected the bond discussed in prenatal class to be a clear-cut *feeling*. After all, attachment is critical, I'd heard. Other young moms raved about it. I assumed all good parents felt a bond to their baby. But the feeling I expected didn't automatically arrive. Oh sure, I wanted and treasured my baby. After months of kicks, hiccups, elbows in my gut, and mysterious companionship, it was incredible to see this tiny person. But recovering from surgery (a cesarean) dampened my euphoria. I didn't *feel* much of anything—except the incision pain. So I waited for a particular emotion.

Late at night as the hospital quieted, I became alert to a persistent, familiar cry from down the corridor. Soon a nurse appeared pushing the clear bassinette holding my cherished possession into my room. I peeled off layers of hospital-certified blankets and was awed at her. I marveled at how she could have coiled inside my womb. I questioned what could go through her tiny mind. The family resemblance was unmistakable. Her face looked like my grandfather's in boyhood photos. Her thumb, a replica of my dad's. Her big toe, just like mine. The complexion of a Nixon, blue eyes, fuzzy head, and dimples when she appeared to gently smile. The smell of my newborn daughter became enjoyable. Her weight in my arms—comfortable. It was ecstasy to quietly sit with her nuzzled into my chest. And, doubting myself, I waited for that imagined sensation to signal my bond with her.

> Look not mournfully into the past; it comes not back. Wisely improve the present.
>
> Longfellow

We proudly and anxiously brought her home. The long haul of nighttime feedings and diaper changes lay before us. First laughs, first cereal, first teeth, and first steps quickly arrived. Then the blur of sick days that seemed too long, and glorious Christmas mornings that seemed too short. A trike, a bike, first grade, school plays, and slumber parties soon filled our lives. Other expectations emerged—some reasonable, some not, yet I never attained that imagined emotion.

Through the years I learned many lessons from parenting. One of the first: bonding isn't an *emotion* but a sense of *knowing* another person. My bond with my daughter is reflected through loving interaction and sharing mutual experiences. That cannot happen in a moment; it must be nurtured over years. If only I had known, I would have recognized that our bond was growing all along, and then no disillusioned expectation would have robbed me of confidence and contentment right from the start.

My Success Strategy

Bonding is happening with my baby when . . .

the wonders of mother's milk

New parents have a zillion decisions to make regarding their child. One of the first choices is whether or not to breast-feed.

Throughout history, parents have maneuvered a labyrinth of advice in their quest to do the right thing. It has almost become a social decision reflecting each generation's lifestyle. In the 1800s, women were told to breast-feed because most alternatives proved fatal. By the 1880s, breast-feeding was seen as indecent because hygiene was better understood and feminism was gaining ground. In her 1896 book *The Way They Should Go,* Mrs. Panton told women to refrain from condemning themselves to nursing like "common cows." Then Truby King's "Breast Fed Is Best Fed" crusade of the 1920s made breast-feeding valued once again. The medical community of the 1950s wasn't as supportive or knowledgeable as the medical community today. My mother was at a loss; she said she never received education or encouragement from her doctor. By the 1980s, super-sensitivity to women's choices turned breast-feeding into an optional war. Today the American Dietetic Association (ADA) promotes and supports breast-feeding as "a public health strategy."[1] So what's a mom to do?

Fortunately, in this information age, medical science offers proof of many baby benefits from mother's milk. Perhaps this might make your decision easier to make. Years ago, a study tracked over one thousand New Zealand children from birth to age eighteen for the purpose of learning about the benefits of breast milk. The study, published in the January 1998 issue of *Pediatrics*, suggested that mom's milk promoted brain development and increased IQ and, ultimately, school success.[2] Its authors, professors at Christchurch School of Medicine, said that fatty acids in human milk are responsible for stimulating brain development. The 2007 *Journal of Nutrition* reports that there is progress in promoting breast-feeding and that manufacturers are trying to modify the composition and quality of formula.[3]

> Over the past twenty-five years, qualitative changes have been made in infant formulas as an attempt to imitate more closely the nutrient structure of human milk.
>
> Brenda Nixon

In regards to premature infants, one study revealed that those who were tube-fed human milk scored higher on developmental tests than those who were formula fed. The study concluded that premature infants receive benefits from breast milk that they can't get from formula.

The current American Academy of Pediatrics (AAP) breast-feeding policy is exclusive breast-feeding for the first six months and support for nursing for the first year as long as mutually desired by mother and child. The AAP agrees with researchers that human milk stimulates infant brain development. Further, the AAP finds evidence that breast-feeding may offer protection against sudden infant death syndrome (SIDS).

Your breasts produce colostrum in the first days after birth. This special, rich milk, which some call "liquid gold," is low in fat and high in carbohydrates, protein, vitamins, and antibodies to help keep your baby healthy. It's extremely easy to digest and is therefore the perfect first food for your newborn.

By the third or fourth day after childbirth, your breasts produce mature milk, which will increase in volume and appear thinner and lighter in color than colostrum. The nourishing mature milk has higher proportions of carbohydrate and fat. The body produces milk in response to demand—the greater the demand, the greater the supply.

An added wonder of breast milk is that each ingredient has its own purpose. For example, particular amino acids, not found in formula, are a core component for the eye's retina development. This could explain why breast-fed babies have better visual acuity. Mother's milk is so precise and complex that no scientist has yet duplicated it. In fact, formula makers are adding some amino acids but admit that their effort will always be an imitation.

Research reports that breast-feeding also gives passive and potentially long-lasting resistance to certain infections. Acute diarrhea, ear infections, and respiratory and urinary tract infections are among those thwarted by human milk. You'd be wise to continue nursing for as long as possible because for each week of nursing, resistance to infections improves.

What are the mom benefits to breast-feeding? Obviously when you nurse, you must hold your baby. This skin-to-skin contact has multiple benefits, such as strengthening the parent/child bond. Research indicates that nursing can reduce your risk of several medical conditions, including ovarian and breast cancer, and possibly decrease the risk of hip fractures and osteoporosis in the postmenopausal period.

Although there are a multitude of benefits, not every mother chooses, or has a situation enabling her, to breast-feed. Some medical conditions complicate or prevent nursing. And certainly loving, nurturing parents can raise intelligent, healthy children using formula. Many factors affect your child's overall development. Having a choice is sometimes a luxury and sometimes a liability. I encourage you to think for yourself and do what is best for your family. But, given the long-term benefits and returns, it is worth trying mother's milk first.

My Success Strategy

I will not let other people dictate such an intimate decision. Whether I breast-feed or not, I will consider the pros and cons of each nutritional method and wholeheartedly choose to . . .

grow a reader

Laura, now twenty years old, confessed recently that she loved the book *Jamberry*. She remembers the silly rhyming text with the dancing bear and little lad as they jam in Berryland, cavort in strawberry fields, rumble and ramble in blackberry brambles, and topple their canoeberry with blueberries. Reading aloud to Laura brought us together for moments of joy and unique mother-daughter bonding.

Right from the start, read aloud to your baby. "Reading aloud is one of the most important parenting activities you can perform," says school psychologist Wesley Sharpe.[1] In repeated studies, reading aloud is the one variable found to have an impact on children's school success. Did you know reading aloud to kids helps them improve in math and social studies? But don't fret now about your child learning to read; more important is first nurturing his awareness of books. Literacy will come. Laura entered kindergarten unable to read. She learned, and today is in college studying to be a teacher.

Your baby must first be accustomed to being around books. He will develop a love for them as he hears the rhythms of your voice and the language, enjoys the warmth and nurturing that comes with your undivided attention, and connects feelings for the book with the most important person in his life. Your baby will learn how books work by watching you turn pages and soon discover that print has purpose. His language skills will be stimulated because reading uses more complex sentence structure than normal talking. As with a muscle, you exercise and stretch his attention span each time you offer a book that engages him. His experiences must be concrete—touching, seeing, hearing. In time, you will see him reach out for the same book you read to him and finger it, showing his desire to be near the book. In later years, he will feel competent enough to tackle the printed word and eager to unlock new information.

Equip your baby now with the right tools. At birth, simplicity is the key. Select stiff cardboard books, soft vinyl books, or cloth books. No words are necessary; black and white images are easier to focus on, especially in the first weeks. There is evidence that patterns enhance a baby's vision. When your baby reaches two months, choose picture books with simple images set against a contrasting background or outlined in black. You can open these books flat and stand them at the side of his crib or, during the day when he's having a bit of floor time on his stomach, place the book on the floor so he can see it. By six to twelve months, he's organized his auditory world and has memory recognition. Choose chunky board, block, or chubby books plus give him old magazines for examination. Because he's developing hand and wrist flexibility, he'll love to manipulate the book and its hinge action. He can sit up with support and hold a book, which is great for banging, dropping, and waving. Books with animal

Simon & Schuster's 1942 book *The Pokey Little Puppy* is now the best-selling picture book of all time.

themes usually interest older babies because animals are one of the first developmental interests outside of Mom and Dad. All babies will crush, rip, and chew pages, so be sure the books are indestructible.

You can also influence his love of literature by letting him see you read your Bible, the newspaper, a recipe, a favorite novel, or the mail. During car trips, read aloud the road signs and billboards. Build a child library by collecting stiff, cardboard books at garage sales and investing in low-cost ones on sale at your public library, and asking family to give books for gifts.

Some of your baby's first books can include *All Fall Down*; *Clap Hands*; *Say Goodnight*; and *Tickle Tickle* by Helen Oxenbury; *Brown Bear, Brown Bear, What Do You See?* by Bill Martin, Jr.; *Goodnight Moon* by Margaret Wise Brown; *Pat the Bunny* by Dorothy Kunhardt; *The Toddler's Bible* by V. Gilbert Beers; and *The Very Hungry Caterpillar* by Eric Carle. "A good story is one that children can touch and feel with their imagination," says Sharpe. "When children travel on imaginary flights they use the mysterious and artistic side of their brain where feelings, emotions, dreams and creativity are born."[2]

As you read aloud, build these important habits:

- Be receptive to his cues. Any time he shows an interest in a book or hands one to you, respond by reading it.
- Spend time with the cover. Say the title, pointing to words as you go.
- Be relaxed. If he senses tension in the muscles of your arms or lap and in your voice, he won't relate reading to pleasure.
- Read slowly. Reading isn't a race; allow time for him to absorb each distinct word. One of my favorite

cartoons, showing a boy and his dad with a book, has the child saying, "Read slower, Daddy. I can't listen that fast."

- Point to pictures as you read. This helps him connect what he hears with what he sees.
- Treat books as a best friend you enjoy seeing repeatedly. Rather than grumble, "We've read that book too many times, let's read something else," say, "Here's *Jamberry*—your favorite! Let's read it again."
- Listen to him when he babbles in pretend-read. He thinks he's copying you in reading, and this is a precursor to successful reading.
- Allow him to wiggle and giggle. Reading is fun and enjoyable, not a sit-still chore.
- Talk to him during the story. Conversations about the book make the experience powerful and personal.
- Get Dad involved. Because females make up 90 percent of the elementary teaching staffs, children often associate reading with women and schoolwork.

For both my daughters, books were companions. I stashed them in the car's glove compartment, toted them to the grocery store and doctor appointments, and scattered them throughout our home. One of my favorite pictures is of curly-haired little Lynsey sitting on her potty chair and looking through a book. Many parents have shared their quiet telephone tip. They keep picture books handy to grab when an important call comes in and they don't want their baby noisily fussing.

What book do you remember reading as a child? Why do you remember that book? Challenge yourself and other adults at home to daily read to your baby. He's not too young—and will never be too old—to be read to.

Children don't learn to love books by themselves. Someone has to lure them into the wonderful world of the written word; someone has to show them the way—that someone can be you.

Perhaps when your child is older, he will call you blessed and pay tribute with a poem similar to American poet and humorist Strickland Gillilan, who penned the famous "The Reading Mother." In the last stanza he shares,

> You may have tangible wealth untold;
> Caskets of jewels and coffers of gold.
> Richer than I you can never be—
> I had a Mother who read to me.

My Success Strategy

My baby will love books—and eventually become a reader—when I show my love for them. Today I will cuddle up with my baby and spend time reading . . .

before regrets, cover outlets

"She's so quick, I turn my back for a minute . . ."

"He's crawling now . . . into everything!"

"No matter what, it goes in his mouth."

I frequently hear these comments from concerned parents in my audiences. And since most accidents occur in the home, here are a few "words to the wise" that may save you some regrets.

Before your child is mobile, childproof your home. Mobile means rolling (three to five months), reaching for things, scooting, crawling, and pulling up to standing (five to eight months), walking and climbing low objects (eight to fourteen months).

One way to childproof is to get on the floor. Now, look around the room through your tot's innocent, adventuresome eyes. *That would be an interesting place to stick my tongue,* imagines a curious baby spying an electrical outlet. *Can I put this over my head like Mom's necklace?* wonders a tot grabbing the mini-blind cord. *Where does this end?* questions an infant pulling on a lamp cord. Every year fifty thousand children are injured from contact with electrical fixtures, cords, and other household equipment.

While on the floor, do you see small objects embedded in your carpet? Pick them up. Between five and eight months of age, all babies are charmed by and will grab tiny things. Of course those immediately go into their mouth. When I'm visiting with the parent of a baby this age, I'll demonstrate her attraction to small objects to raise awareness of this danger. I ask the parent to place her baby's favorite book, toy, or stuffed animal on the floor next to Baby. Then I'll get a small item like a thumbtack from my pocket and lay it next to Baby. We watch, and even with age-appropriate toys surrounding her, she'll reach for the tack, much to Mom's horror. Of course, I immediately snatch the dangerous object away and offer an appropriate toy. But the point is clearly made.

During babyhood months, be alert and hunt for seemingly insignificant items on the floor that would eventually end up in your baby's mouth. Never leave her unsupervised anywhere, especially in the bathroom where pills, hairpins, and other small objects may be unnoticeably lying on the floor. And anything in her mouth can go down and wedge in her flexible throat, which stretches up to one and a half inches in diameter.

Don't give her small, hard foods like peanuts. Until she is seven years old, when she masters the mechanics of chewing, she can choke on seemingly harmless treats. I know a mom whose tot died after choking on a piece of sausage. Your best preparation for a potentially tragic scenario is infant CPR.

Be a good detective as you search for and correct potential home hazards. Hide or tape up all cords; remove pole lamps; and move plants, breakables, and handbags to a level out of your tot's reach. Many poisonings occur when inquisitive tots get into handbags containing medications or vitamins.

Write the poison control number on every telephone along with other emergency contacts. This saves time and thought when you're in a panic over what your little one put in her mouth.

In 1965, the Food and Drug Administration (FDA) approved syrup of ipecac as an over-the-counter remedy for accidental poisonings. The American Academy of Pediatrics (AAP), the American Association of Poison Control Centers, the American Medical Association (AMA), and the Medical Advisory Board of the FDA agreed on its use for more than forty years. When Lynsey and Laura were babies, syrup of ipecac was a household staple. Hospitals even gave it away to new parents. However, it has since fallen out of favor because it wasn't associated with improvement in patient outcome. Side effects sometimes included drowsiness, lethargy, and diarrhea. Ipecac syrup removed about one-third of the stomach's contents, but only if it was given within the first hour after ingestion of a substance. In some cases prolonged vomiting occurred, but there was no reduction in the substance. So, in 2003, the AAP announced that syrup of ipecac no longer had a place in the home management of poisoning and recommended that parents no longer keep it on hand. Later the same year, the Nonprescription Drug Advisory Panel of the FDA recommended removal of ipecac syrup as over-the-counter (OTC) status.

> It may seem like a lot to do, but childproofing happens in stages, just as a baby's development occurs in stages.
>
> Cindy Wolf

Keep the lid down on toilets. All young children are top-heavy and easily fall headfirst into open toilets, bathtubs, buckets, and other sources of contained water. When they get their face under water they often lack upper body strength or judgment to lift up to breathe. Residential pools pose the highest water danger to tots on the move.

Inspect your baby's toys to insure they are lightweight, washable, and have no sharp edges that could slice tender gums. Beware of rummage sale finds as older toys may not pass today's safety standards of lead-free paints. Older clothes may not be flame retardant.

Get into the habit now of turning pot handles in toward the middle of your stove; place guards over heaters and in front of fireplaces; and keep hot liquids away from the table's edge. I know a baby girl who was rushed to the emergency room after pulling the tablecloth and dumping Mom's scalding coffee down onto her face. Burns send thousands of tots to the hospital every year because their thinner skin is more vulnerable to scalding than that of older kids and adults.

Today there are ways to fully protect your baby around home fireplaces. Custom Baby Safety Fireplace Hearth Guard is an easy-to-install foam that covers your entire hearth—not just the edges. Read about it at www.babysafetyfoam.com.

There are over twenty free PDF and HTML brochures on safety proofing available to you from the U.S. Consumer Product Safety Commission at www.cpsc.gov/cpscpub/pubs/chld_sfy.html. Several brochures are translated into Spanish too.

My Success Strategy

To ensure my baby's safety and my peace of mind, today I'm going to . . .

quality childcare checklist

I've been a full-time, stay-at-home mom, a stay-at-home mom with a home business, and the parent who goes out to work. The most exhausting—and often the loneliest—was the first. Yet, I embraced it, read parenting books, studied the latest research, and worked on a healthy relationship with my daughter. For me, it was—still is—important to be as conscientious and committed to parenting as to any other career. I want my children to know they come first in my life.

However, there came a point in early parenthood when family finances required I earn income in the labor force. Although I was creative in saving and budgeting money, Paul and I just couldn't crunch the numbers enough, and we needed two sets of wages.

So, I sought out quality childcare for our precious daughter. The better the childcare, the more I could relax, and the better off my child would be in many ways.

Childcare is becoming a critical issue for parents because the number of women in the workforce has nearly doubled in just twenty-five years, and many employers do not offer on-site daycare. Instead of parents providing early childcare, it is outsourced. A 2007 Census Bureau report shows married mothers of infants comprise 53.3 percent of the labor force.[1] As a result, on a routine basis, someone other than Mom is caring for over half the babies under one year of age.

Consider this statistic: when Mom joins the workforce, up to 68 percent of her income goes for work-related expenses, such as childcare, transportation, taxes, and lunch money.[2] Quality childcare will take a big bite out of your earned income. To determine if your family can afford a stay-at-home parent, compute the costs using the calculator at http://life.familyeducation.com/calculator/stay-at-home-cost/55187.html?detoured=1.

> Research proves that parents have an important influence on their child's development regardless of how much out-of-home care the child receives.
>
> Brenda Nixon

The decision about whether to stay home or work outside the home is yours, and you may be a single parent without an option. My advice is to do what's right for your family in your particular situation and be prepared for the pros and cons of the decision. "Life is about choices. And each choice brings with it a price tag, a sacrifice—something that must be given up or postponed," says Trish Berg in her book *Rattled: Surviving Your Baby's First Year Without Losing Your Cool.*[3]

If you're in the market for quality childcare, shop around as carefully as you would for any other major investment. From safety and setting, to staff and story time, know the key elements of quality care. Be an educated consumer on behalf of your most valuable possession. If you already have a childcare arrangement, evaluate it against these criteria. Look for a center or private home where:

- *It's generally clean, well lit, and ventilated.* The play area should be cluttered with toys, but it can still look and smell clean. A well-lighted play area promotes your youngster's eye-hand skill. Good ventilation prevents recycling the same old germs. But expect a seasonal cold or flu when tots come in close contact with each other at daycare.

- *It is a safe environment.* The National Association for the Education of Young Children (NAEYC) in Washington, DC, suggests that staff should be well versed in health and safety procedures and be able to describe the policy for handling emergencies. In a safe environment, children will be under adult supervision at all times.
- *Parents feel comfortable asking questions.* If you ask several questions and the caregivers seem offended or avoid your inquisition, leave. If they are knowledgeable and proud of the facility, they will be eager to share.
- *Parents are told to drop in anytime.* You want to make sure that caregivers welcome parents for lunch, special activities, or just to observe.
- *Parenting literature and child development resources are available.* Your tot deserves an environment where parent education and professional growth are encouraged. Remember, great minds are always learning.
- *Toys and play equipment are child sized, age appropriate, and regularly maintained and cleaned.* Tables and chairs must be small enough so kids can sit at the table without their feet dangling. It's a chiropractic nightmare when children sit on big chairs straining their toes to touch the floor, as this puts undue pressure on the spine.
- *Pictures and room decor are down on the child's eye level.* Keep in mind, this is a place for children, not adults.
- *Adult turnover is low.* A steady stream of new caregivers distresses youngsters. It may signal to you that

a relationship problem exists between staff and the director, a problem that trickles down to your child.

- *Children are touched appropriately, frequently, and in positive, affirming ways.* Children need to be touched, even if it's a pat on the back, or holding hands during games.
- *Each child is addressed by name.* Listen for a minimal use of group terms like "the infants," "babies," or "kids."
- *There's equal attention to cognitive, social, emotional, and physical development.* According to the NAEYC website (www.naeyc.org), "High quality early childhood programs do much more than help children learn numbers, shapes, and colors. Good programs help children learn how to learn: to question why and discover alternative answers; to get along with others; and to use their developing language, thinking, and motor skills."
- *Caregivers are trained in early childhood education.* They should participate in annual continuing education and meet regularly to plan and evaluate their program.
- *There's a low adult/child ratio.* The NAEYC recommends at least one caregiver for every

  four infants (birth to twelve months)

  five younger toddlers (twelve to twenty-four months)

  six older toddlers (two to three years)

  Smaller groups or a lower adult/child ratio have been found to promote more positive interactions and more individualized curriculum.
- *Childrearing and discipline philosophies are similar to your own.* You want to leave your child in an

environment consistent with your home discipline. Ask "what if" questions to be sure.

- *Sign-in and -out policies are enforced.* Especially if you leave your little one in a large center with lots of foot traffic, security precautions are a must.
- *It's either certified or licensed by your state.* Certification and/or licensure gives you a minimum health, safety, and nutritional standard—not a guarantee it's the right place for your child. I've known some licensed facilities where I wouldn't leave my dog. Neither does certification or licensure limit curriculum; church-run facilities can be licensed and still teach religious curriculum.

A word to the wise: be wary of the caregiver with the "Honey, I've been tendin' kids for twenty years, an' I know all there is to raisin' babies!" attitude. A caregiver worth his or her salt—and your money—needs to learn about your child and continually sharpen caregiving skills.

Finally, check with your local health department and Better Business Bureau to see if the place you're considering has a record of complaints. Remember, knowledge is power.

Research proves that parents have an important influence on their child's development regardless of how much out-of-home care the child receives. Whether you are at home or work outside the home, you are still your child's most important teacher.

My Success Strategy

In looking for quality childcare I'm going to ask these questions . . .

starting solid foods

According to my baby album, Mom plugged me with cereal when I was four weeks old. It was the "she'll sleep through the night" mentality. When I was eight weeks old, she put me on whole (yes!) milk laced with Karo syrup. Soon after, according to my baby book, she proudly penned that I was eating fruits and veggies. "Karo taken out at ten weeks" my loving mom dutifully recorded.

Now, that was the post–World War II "as God is my witness my kid'll never go hungry" era. And Mom did whatever her doctor, equivalent to God, told her. Today, however, parents have more pediatric coaching and education on when to start solids. Information opportunities abound through county health departments and education programs like "Healthy Families" and "Parents as Teachers."

It's normal for new parents to crave a good night's sleep in those first weeks with an infant. This period can seem endless. But sleep has less to do with a full tummy than a baby's nervous system development. So don't fall for the myth that giving nighttime cereal will help your baby sleep. In fact, feeding cereal too soon may backfire; with a bloated stomach, some babies become more fidgety and wake frequently.

Today, most experts agree that four weeks is too young for solid foods. Remember, in the first weeks of life an infant cannot hold up his head, making it difficult to swallow anything more than liquid. Also, the immature digestive system is unable to handle solids. "Before they're three to four months old, babies automatically push out their tongues when anything enters their mouths. This reaction, called the extrusion reflex, is essential for breast-feeding and bottle-feeding, and it indicates that infants can swallow only liquids," write the authors of the article "Introducing Solid Foods: What You Need to Know" at MayoClinic.com.[1]

> In infants, milk products and eggs are the most common food allergies.
>
> Dr. Michael LaCombe

Yet, don't wait a year to introduce solids. "Some babies not started on solids by a certain age (nine to twelve months) may have great difficulty accepting solid foods," cautions pediatrician and author Dr. Jack Newman.[2]

So how do you know when to supplement solid food alongside milk? Like many other milestones in parenting, there's more than age to consider. Wait until your baby shows signs of being ready, and don't depend on the calendar age.

First, watch for sturdy neck muscles that can hold up his head. This will make swallowing easier. Usually, a strong neck is common in his fourth or fifth month. About this same time, his digestive system is mature enough to tolerate solids, and the extrusion reflex is gone.

Around six months, most babies begin to sit up. Some can do it alone, but many still rely on a little support. They're better at transferring food from the front of their tongue to the back, which makes swallowing a bit more graceful and successful.

Proper food introduction is imperative for infants. Cereal is recommended as the first food because it's mild and easy to digest. Many pediatricians suggest rice cereal as it may be less allergy producing than the others.

When Lynsey was about six months old, I'd prop her up on our sofa. Then I'd kneel down in front of her with a bowl of slightly warm baby cereal and her small padded spoon. Sometimes I'd sit her in an infant carrier to feed her. Our first attempts were muddled and messy, but within days, Lynsey (and I) got the hang of it. Then she'd open wide like a little chick waiting for its mama.

On your first attempt to spoon feed, be prepared for a mess. Many babies will eject the cereal; their tongue is unfamiliar with a spoon. Some have trouble knowing how much to swallow—that's why it's better to use baby spoons. If your baby isn't interested, quit for the moment. Simply wipe off his face and try again later. Make the first try at solid food a pleasant one. Don't push or insist that he eat all his cereal.

When your baby is consistently holding up his head and starting to sit up, you can place dry, unsweetened, O-shaped cereal in front of him. This will give him opportunities to pick it up and feed himself, which requires a great deal of coordination but is necessary to practice.

"At about eight months of age, babies become somewhat assertive in displaying their individuality," explains Newman. "Your baby may not want you to put a spoon into his mouth. He very likely will take it out of your hand and put it into his mouth himself, often upside down, so that the food falls on his lap."[3] Encouraging these attempts at self-sufficiency builds your baby's self-esteem. Although it can be a complete mess for you, be happy and relieved that he's wanting to grow up.

By nine months, look for your baby to pinch his index finger and thumb together. Now, he can easily pick up small items. His hand-to-mouth coordination is improving. At this age, you can lay small cooked vegetable strips, peeled soft fruit, or cheese cubes out for your baby. It takes practice to learn how much food to bite off, chew, and swallow. Learning to eat solid foods is a milestone in child development. Always supervise your tot during mealtimes to prevent choking.

One day when Lynsey was around twelve months old, she was munching her favorite food—cooked broccoli (at twenty-five she still loves it). I watched as she gently picked up each tender, tiny shoot of the softened green and put it in her mouth. With bulging chipmunk cheeks my daughter picked up another, then another. I watched her chew and reach out for more pieces. Then I noticed she had not swallowed. "Lynsey, swallow your food," I said. She looked at me. "Swallow," I repeated. My little daughter couldn't. She had more in her mouth than her throat could accommodate. "Spit it out," I urged. Lynsey bent over her plate and opened up. Out fell enough broccoli to build a tree house. Thankfully, she didn't swallow. The large amount could've caused a blockage, subsequent choking, or even death.

Expect topsy-turvy meals for many months. By the first birthday, your baby will probably grab the spoon and feed himself. He may want a spoon in each hand. This too is a messy experience, but he needs to learn. And learning only comes with practice and patience. To relieve my anxiety over messy floors and faces, I often laid a plastic drop cloth under my girls' high chair. After each was done, I wiped fingers and faces then removed her from the chair. Next, I picked up the drop cloth and went to the trashcan to shake off the excess or wiped it clean for next time.

Introducing foods is the beginning of new adventures. I have a photo of young Lynsey sitting at the table. Over her face and into her hairline is tomato sauce. She was feeding herself ravioli—truly a face only a mother could love!

My Success Strategy

Eating solid food is a new experience for me and my baby. To be calmly prepared I will . . .

soothe separation anxiety

Lynsey wrapped her chubby, short arms around my leg and cried, “No-no-no!” as I tried to leave the church nursery. It nearly tore out my heart to hear her sobs, but I knew it was a part of her development.

Between eight to ten months of age, your baby may start a painful stage of development. These past months she has become increasingly attached to you as you’ve met her needs on a daily basis. She has also been so new to the world that she’s had little knowledge of what was ordinary, so new situations or experiences seemed usual, not frightening. Now when you leave her at daycare or with Grandpa and Grandma or a trusted friend, she suddenly starts crying. Big tears roll down her round cheeks, and her lower lip rolls out and quivers. You sense she feels anxious, and that parental instinct kicks in. You reach out to take her back into your arms and whisper, “I’m here. It’s all right.” She calms as you wipe away the tears. Then she turns back into the happy little girl you know. You hand her over to the other pair of arms, and she winds up again like a siren.

Separation anxiety is a normal, albeit painful, development milestone that helps children learn how to master their environment. You might see it last until fourteen months, and differ among children. Laura expressed her anxiety more passionately than Lynsey. When she wailed I went to war within myself; my head said that she'd be fine, but my heart screamed, "Go get her!"

> Healing is a matter of time, but it is sometimes also a matter of opportunity.
> Hippocrates

There's good and bad news about the onset of separation anxiety. The good news is that you've done nothing wrong. If you're employed outside the home and leave your baby in the arms of another, you are not making it worse or better. If you are a stay-at-home parent you are not making it worse or better. It is a stage of development as natural as learning to walk.

Actually, your baby is experiencing a burst of development in two areas. She's experiencing more long-term memory, or what experts call cognitive growth. What was once "out of sight, out of mind" is now "out of sight and still in mind." The thought of you leaving her sight is causing her grief. She is quite sensitive now to the comings and goings of the important people in her life. Separation isn't pleasant for any of us, and it's a new, nerve-racking emotion for a tot learning to cope with Mom or Dad's absence.

Expanding social skills is the second root of this issue. As part of her social maturation, she's discovering that she needs you, but she also wants to detach. This inner dependence versus independence conflict can be quite troubling.

The bad news is that separation anxiety has to take its sweet time to blossom, wither, and pass away. Then it may bloom briefly during periods of stress such as starting a new preschool or entering kindergarten.

You can skillfully facilitate your baby's ability to cope with separation now and in the future by playing games. At home, hide a favorite toy under a blanket then "find" it together, or play peek-a-boo often. These simple social activities have more value than just entertainment. Both teach your baby that her world is predictable and safe.

Next tell yourself that separation anxiety is natural, and your response can make it worse or better. The better way to soothe separation anxiety is to simply confront it. Give your baby a reassuring hug and kiss before you hand her over to your caregiver. Say, "I will be back," turn, and leave. Some daycares have a "good-bye window" where parent and child may wave to one another.

Prevent sabotaging your baby's opportunity to mature and separate by resisting the urge to

- *Linger.* If you hang around, you send a message that you're unsure about her ability to cope with separation. She will muddle through in time and with practice. Hippocrates said, "Healing is a matter of time, but it is sometimes also a matter of opportunity."
- *Sneak out.* If you creep away unnoticed, you send a message that you're not a predictable parent. Your child will live in vague suspicion that you'll disappear again, and she'll "guard" you, afraid to leave your side to play. While sneaking away is easier for you, it's ultimately not good for your baby.
- *Patronize.* To say "You shouldn't cry" only demeans, rather than respects, her anxiety.
- *Rush in to rescue.* If, within minutes, you come back to scoop up your crying daughter, she learns to cry until you return. This will develop a conditioned behavior. Give her time to self-calm.

It is skillful parenting to accept separation anxiety as a challenge, while remembering it's a part of growing and learning to handle new feelings. Your baby is remarkably resilient; with your respect, comfort, and care, she'll learn to cope with loss now and in the future. Now, that's a valuable life skill.

My Success Strategy

When my baby cries with separation anxiety it will be uncomfortable for me. But now that I know it's a phase, I can help my child move through it by . . .

your child's expert

She was frantic. With trembling in her voice, a mom phoned my office to say, "My daughter is almost eleven months old, and she's still not sitting up without a lot of support. I know children develop at different rates, but this seems very far behind to me. We've recently changed pediatricians, and the new one says not to worry but hasn't given a clear idea of when might be a good time to be concerned. Could you please give an age range of when I should start to worry if she isn't sitting up without support?"

"Always trust your gut," I advised. "You know your daughter better than anyone else, and if you feel concerned, then you're right in campaigning for her." Since parents live with their child, I feel they are their child's expert. They are wise to team up with pediatricians and developmental specialists to understand their child's maturity and then take an active role in supporting their child's progress.

According to the Denver Development Screen Tool (DDST), a standardized assessment used in many school districts, preschools, and hospitals, a baby should sit without support between five and seven months of age. In fact, if she can't master this skill at eleven months old, as this mom described, then there may be a gross motor delay. World-renowned pediatrician and author Dr. T. Berry Brazelton says that a baby of nine months can get from her belly into a sitting position. So certainly, the complex motor skills involved in sitting are to be mastered at eleven months of age.

> I really learned it all from mothers.
>
> Dr. Benjamin Spock

In my work with parents, I find that sometimes a delay is a lack of opportunity. Perhaps parents constantly carry their baby and forget to give him "floor time" or they always prop up their baby with pillows or other back support. Then their baby doesn't have the opportunity to sit unaided, fall over, and try again. When you have your baby supported in a seated position, remove the support and see if he can sustain an upright position. Practice makes permanent.

When you have a question about your baby's development, discuss it with his pediatrician. If you feel your concern is not valued and addressed, change doctors. Also, check your state's Department of Health, the local school districts, or hospitals to see if they know of a free program called "Parents As Teachers." This international parent education program gives developmental information to parents plus performs periodic developmental screenings on young children in the privacy of your home. You might want to enroll in it and take advantage of the information, support, and new friendships gained. To find a local Parents As Teachers program, go to their national center website at www.patnc.org. Also, review my developmental guide in appendix B of this book.

Raising a baby brings many questions and uncertainties. Skillful parents observe their child and aren't afraid to ask questions, to learn, and to be their child's advocate throughout life. I hope this helps you go forward with confidence.

My Success Strategy

My baby needs me as an advocate for him when I have a concern over his development. To empower myself I want to read books on this topic, including . . .

self-esteem is taught

Parents with low self-esteem often express concern to me that they fear their child will have low self-esteem too. Self-esteem, low or high, is not inherited; it is learned. And it is learned from the first and most influential teachers—Mom and Dad.

But what if I don't have good self-esteem? you worry. There are simple yet profound ways to teach your tot that she is valued, wanted, and respected. At this tender age, you can already nurture her understanding and respect for herself.

If your infant is under six months, try doing these things every day:

Hold her when you feed her with a bottle. She must feel loving arms around her, to see you giving full attention to her nutritive need. Propping up a bottle with pillows to feed a baby increases the risk of ear infection, and it's pretty impersonal too. For most of us, eating is a social time. We enjoy our food more when in the company of loved ones.

Immediately respond to her cries. Infants cry when they are in discomfort—not to infuriate you. When they need food, warmth, or quiet, their primary way of expression is through the mouth. By responding quickly and calmly, you teach your baby that her needs are recognized and valid. And you are helping her develop a trust relationship with you. In fact, trust is one of the major developmental tasks in the first year of life.

> I love little children, and it is not a slight thing when they, who are fresh from God, love us.
>
> Charles Dickens

Parents who always respond with impatience or anger send the message to their child that she is a nuisance. This causes her to grow up feeling apologetic for her needs. You may know an adult today who begins nearly every sentence with, "I'm sorry to disturb you, but . . ."

When you pick up your baby, name her feelings. Something like, "You're feeling tired now," or "That noise frightened you," is descriptive. It helps your little one gradually recognize and name her emotions. A core component of self-esteem is the ability to be in touch with and express one's emotions. With teaching like this, later in life she'll more likely express herself with words instead of actions.

Daily look in the mirror together. For now, she just sees another image—not another baby. Over time she will come to understand that the image looking back belongs to her. Be sure to smile when you look in the mirror as this is contagious as well as relaxing.

Frequently repeat your baby's name. Hearing her name helps her become accustomed to its sound and attach it to her identity.

Read aloud to your baby. "But," you say, "she can't understand a thing I'm reading." True. But she sure enjoys you wanting to be near her, your soothing voice, your touch, your undivided attention. By reading to her, you casually nurture a love for the written word while sending a message that she is a lovable human being.

Several times each day, place her on the floor. Giving her floor space to freely move about will encourage her to use her muscles and build her upper-body strength. This respects her growing body and need to explore.

When your baby is six to twelve months old, it's helpful to:

Begin naming her body parts to her. Some parents make up songs involving the names of the body. Some parents like to play simple games like "I Got Your Nose." The value of doing this is to teach your tot her uniqueness apart from you.

Use positive discipline such as redirection. One mother asked me when she should start slapping her son's hands. Why discourage curiosity and a drive to learn? When your baby reaches for something that is off limits, direct her attention to another acceptable object. Babies of this age have a short attention span, so it's easy to engage them in other, more appropriate activities.

Stick with routine bath, bed, and meal times. If possible, try to do the same things with her every day. Although it sounds boring to us, babies feel secure and thrive when their life is comfortably predictable.

Allow her to hold her own cup and drink. While this may be messy, it gives her practice. Soon she will feel capable of doing things for herself. Feeling capable is another key component of self-esteem.

Encourage your baby to feed herself. Don't worry about food in the hair, on the table, and on the floor. Learning self-care practices such as feeding herself is a skill that gives her dignity. If given this opportunity, any baby can feed herself by the first birthday.

Expect your child to grab, taste, poke, pour, and dump everything she can get her hands on. These are normal, healthy behaviors of a thriving baby driven by curiosity. And because she is doing these normal things, be one step ahead by safety-proofing her play areas. This will allow her to safely explore and begin testing her independence without constantly hearing, "No!" "Don't," "Put that down," and "Stop!"

Sing songs and play simple games like pat-a-cake and peekaboo. If you don't know many, check out nursery rhyme and songbooks from the public library. "How does this teach self-esteem?" you ask. By proving that the world can be a welcoming place to live and learn.

With your tender teaching, your baby will grow up with the wonderful knowledge that she is lovable and capable, and will be confident in life.

My Success Strategy

I want to build my baby's self-esteem and give her resilience for life's challenges. I can do that by . . .

protect those peepers

The threat is invisible. Your baby's eyes could be victim. Studies show that excessive exposure to bright sunlight may increase the risk of developing cataracts—a clouding of the eye's lens. Unprotected exposure may also increase the risk of macular degeneration and growths on the eye, including cancer, later in life.[1] The longer the exposure to the sun's ultraviolet (UV) rays—an invisible energy—the greater the risk.

Even UV light reflected off sand, snow, water, or pavement can, over time, damage your baby's eyes; and like his skin, eyes never recover from UV exposure. Tots have occasionally exhibited what doctors first thought was an eye infection called conjunctivitis, when in reality their eyeballs were swollen and red due to extreme sun exposure without sunglasses.

Our bodies convert sunlight into vitamin D. So short spurts of sunlight are important for good health. But too much of a good thing is harmful.

Be wise right from the start. Remember, the sun's UV rays pass through haze and thin clouds. Damage to eyes can occur anytime during the year, including cloudy days. According to the American Cancer Society, "Babies younger than six months should be kept out of direct sunlight."[2] If you live or vacation at high altitudes, the UV radiation increases 4 to 5 percent for every one thousand feet above sea level.

So do you protect the eyes with those cute "kiddy" glasses? The American Cancer Society states, "Children need smaller versions of real, protective adult sunglasses—not toy sunglasses."

> Ultraviolet protection doesn't come from the sunglasses' color or darkness but from an invisible chemical applied to the lenses.
>
> Brenda Nixon

Eye specialists believe that toy sunglasses may actually be worse than none at all because toy shades simply darken the eye area and enlarge your tot's pupils, allowing damage to the inside of the eye. Don't be deceived by pretty colors or cartoon characters. The best sunglasses are those simply labeled "100 percent UV filtration." The high price for this full protection pales in comparison to costly or painful eye problems down the road.

I wish I had known this when Lynsey and Laura were babies. Using sunscreen on their skin was a common practice, but unfortunately, I overlooked eye protection.

Today, most parents are convinced of the need to protect delicate eyes during outdoor adventures. But the real trick is keeping sunglasses on a baby. While wearing sunglasses isn't as grave as teaching your tot to stay in a car seat or other safety issues, you do want to encourage their use. Here are four tips to make your job easier:

- Remember the adage "Monkey see, monkey do" and use it to your advantage. Wear funky, fun glasses outdoors and your tot will want to wear some too.
- Buy glasses with large lenses, a snug fit, and a "wraparound" design. Ideally, they should wrap all the way

around to the temples, so the sun's rays can't sneak in from the side. The snug fit helps them stay put when tiny fingers grab at them. Baby sunglasses with soft foam frames and a Velcro strap in the back are now available from Frubi Shades.

- If possible, keep your baby out of direct sunlight between 10:00 a.m. and 3:00 p.m. According to the Federal Trade Commission and the American Academy of Ophthalmology, these are the hours when the sun's damaging rays are highest.[3]
- Keep young hands busy, with simple toys or cool treats like Popsicles, so they aren't pulling off sunglasses.

If your tot is still reluctant and tugs at his eye protection, keep a wide-brimmed hat or bonnet nearby to shade susceptible eyes. While an infant-size baseball cap protects the front and top of the head, it leaves the back of the neck and ears, where skin cancers commonly develop, vulnerable. A floppy cap with material down the sides and back provides more protection.

My Success Strategy

I will start now teaching my baby to protect himself from sun damage by . . .

ten tips for stress-*less* parenting

Stress is anything we perceive to be out of our control. This definition makes sense because we like to feel "things are under control," and it explains why stress differs for each person. Can finances, relatives, and computers be out of our control? Of course. As I write, I wish I could reach into my computer and make it run faster. Likewise, the weather, a screaming infant, traffic, schedules, church, or clutter each represent a potential source of stress. There is a duality of stress. Experts claim that living totally stress free is not good for us (although I would like to try it for a day). Moderate stress sharpens and motivates us to make change, while too much will destroy health and relationships.

Stress differs for moms, dads, and the single parent. Its sources change with the family composition and with the ages and stages of childrearing. As parents, we all have days when we feel our child and her behavior is out of our control. We feel trapped by the constant responsibility, and we worry how she'll turn out. It takes enormous energy to tend to the hourly needs of a growing baby. As a new mom, I thought I had to have all the answers. Well, I didn't, and trying to act as if I did increased stress for my baby and me. Raising a child is a nerve-racking task—not for the faint-hearted. Comedian Martin Mull quipped, "Parenting is like having a bowling alley in your head."

"When you feel stressed, you usually have some physical symptoms," says the Canadian Mental Health Association. "You can feel tired, get headaches, stomach upsets or backaches, clench your jaw or grind your teeth, develop skin rashes, have recurring colds or flu, have muscle spasms or nervous twitches, or have problems sleeping. Mental signs of stress include feeling pressured, having difficulty concentrating, being forgetful, and having trouble making decisions. Emotional signs include feeling angry, frustrated, tense, anxious, or more aggressive than usual."[1]

> If there is no enemy within, the enemy without can do you no harm.
>
> African proverb

On my bad days, I try to remember the words of Albert Einstein, "Not everything that counts can be counted. And not everything that can be counted—counts." This prompts me to relax and stop fretting about every detail in my children's lives or overresponding to the size of a challenge. And despite the challenges, "we need to take comfort in knowing that the good things we try to do as parents really do matter," writes research professor Craig H. Hart of Brigham Young University.[2]

Two characters or words in Chinese spell "stress"; one character means "danger" and the other means "opportunity." I think that perfectly explains the tension in childrearing today; it can be a hazard, but it also gives us opportunities to learn, laugh, grow, and make memories to fall back on when the children are grown and on their own.

Parenting demands enormous time, patience, creativity, faith, and inspiration. In these first years, I hope you'll remember, during the turbulent, out-of-control times, these tips for stress-less parenting. You may not minimize stress, but you can maximize your coping ability. Take a deep breath and repeat to yourself:

- All kids can and do misbehave.
- There are no perfect kids. Wanting the ideal child can get in the way of enjoying the one I have.
- There are no perfect parents.
- This too shall pass. Parenting is a short season of my life.
- There is humor (somewhere) in this situation. Humor has positive effects on my brain by stimulating neurotransmitters that help me relax.
- I can emotionally disconnect. I will take a break through exercise, soothing music, reading a chapter in my favorite book, or sipping a cup of coffee.
- Talking to other adults can ease my loneliness or frustration.
- Wisdom knows what to overlook. Some things just do not count in demanding my attention.
- Good parents practice self-care. I will nurture myself physically, emotionally, and spiritually through good nutrition, sleep, and prayer or meditation.
- I will live a long, happy life and eventually be a problem to my child.

Post this list on your refrigerator as a reminder to "accept the things I cannot change; courage to change the things I can; and wisdom to know the difference."

My Success Strategy

Excess stress can devastate me physically and emotionally and diminish my parenting abilities. For my best parenting right from the start, I'll prevent unnecessary stress by . . .

1

2 parenting your toddler

3

4

father facts

Hey, Dad, this one's for you. (Moms, if you're reading this, show it to your child's father.) You'll be your daughter's first love and your son's earliest role model. Research says that your daily interaction with your kids improves their physical health, IQ, independence, school success, and future relationships.

Studies in both the United States and Europe document the impact a dad has on his child's life. The research reports that how *and* how much of a difference hinges on his time investment and behavior toward his child. One study in Russia showed "that physical and relational aggression directed toward peers at school occurred less frequently when fathers were more patient, responsive, and playful" in their interactions with their children, writes researcher Craig H. Hart.[1]

Evidence suggests that infants are able to make use of a father's unique contribution to their growth and development. Men tend to encourage more exploration, risk taking, and assertiveness in children. The Mom versus Dad parenting differences also appear to be of great interest and benefit to children by creating a balance in their lives.

There are various ways to draw your child into your life and contribute to his. Actor and game show host Ben Stein said, "Go home from work early and spend the afternoon throwing a ball around with your son." Gary Foreman, a south Florida father of two, says he's been involved with his kids from their birth. "We waited twelve years before having kids," Foreman explains. "Now we're kind of old-fashioned. We have family dinners, play board games, my daughter and I go out to garage sales, and I enjoy catching a football with my son." Likewise, Doug Ward of Wheaton, Illinois, says he was an involved dad "from the day we brought them home from the hospital."

> The simple truth is that fathers are irreplaceable in shaping the competence and character of their children.
>
> David Blankenhorn

Every day and in many ways you make a lasting impression on your child. "I want to show my kids how to solve problems," says Foreman. Ward hopes to do more than tell them about "faith and values. I hope that I have shown them." The comedian Bill Cosby said, "If the new American father feels bewildered and even defeated, let him take comfort from the fact that whatever he does in any fathering situation has a 50 percent chance of being right."[2]

Even if you didn't have a strong father role model, you have a great opportunity now to redefine fatherhood for your child. In her book *Rattled*, author Trish Berg lists five ways to be a great dad, including taking some late-night bottle-feeding shifts. Here are other simple, yet profound, ways to connect and make a lasting impression on your child:

- Attend parenting classes and learn about child development.
- Support, protect, and assist the mother/child relationship. Research suggests that your bond with your child

is not likely to be threatened by a stronger maternal attachment.

- Eat family meals at least three times a week. Children have a yearning to be with their dad, so your presence is needed more than your presents.
- Read books to your child. A man's voice brings an interesting quality to reading.
- Be consistent in discipline. Your child will learn that you're a promise keeper.
- Go on family outings. Your budget doesn't matter. A trip to the zoo is as meaningful as an expensive theme park—it's the interaction with your child that counts.
- Play board and card games with your youngster. Playing together builds memories and emotional connections.
- Use your lunch hour to visit his daycare. Just showing up sends a powerful message of the value you place on being with your child.
- Give lots of hugs. This is especially critical as children mature and you naturally touch them less.
- Generously offer verbal encouragement. Your words are often prophetic.

Men never regret being involved in their child's life—although the converse is true. "I would like to think that my time has demonstrated to them how much I love them and made them better able to stand up to greater pressures yet to come," says Ward. To be in your child's happy memories tomorrow, you must be in his life today.

Psychologist John Snarey found that fathers have a profound influence on their child's later life successes. You are shaping the competence and very character of your child by what you do now. Reevaluate how your fathering style is contributing to your child's life and what changes you might make to acknowledge the powerful effect your presence has on your child's future development.

If you are a single mother reading this, don't feel helpless. Find a stable role model. There are people willing to give the positive influence you want for your child. An uncle, grandfather, "Big Brother," or minister can be a mentor in the absence of a dad. As one man wrote, "I never took the time to have children of my own and was fortunate to develop a friendship with someone whose children weren't that interested in terrorizing an adult. . . . My life has been a thousand times better, and I have this funny warm feeling inside when I look back at each little adventure or experience with them. Everyone should have children if they truly want to know what wealth is."

So, Dad, not only will you make a positive imprint on your child's future, but think of it in reverse. How is your child making a positive difference in your life? "Two summers back," remembers one man, "I put rollerblades on and skated for the first time because a child held my hand and was pleased that I was interested in spite of my fear of falling."

Just for fun, look at some other "dads" taking an earnest role in bringing up their young:

- The male penguin "babysits" mom's eggs when she waddles off on a break.
- Male toadfish safeguard their eggs, snapping viciously at anyone coming near.
- The male marmoset cleans his newborn's fur then totes his baby around for the first few months of life.
- Male swans fiercely charge at anyone or anything threatening their young.

- The male Guinea fowl teaches his young how to range and watch for predators—especially the hawks.

For more help on fathering, see the resources listed in appendix C of this book.

My Success Strategy

How am I staying involved in my child's life?

For Mom: I can affirm my child's father and draw him in to the childcare by . . .

ten traits of toddlers

Exasperating, entertaining, and *extraordinary* are among the words used to describe toddlers. Be prepared, toddlerhood is probably the most hair-raising, roller-coaster, thrill ride during your parenthood—until the teen years. What comedian Bill Cosby said of childrearing applies: "You just need a lot of love and luck—and, of course, courage."

Developmentally speaking, a toddler is twelve to thirty-six months of age. While there's a huge maturity gulf between a twelve-month-old and a thirty-six-month-old, these years are clustered together due to similar traits.

Living with a toddler can bankrupt any parent's energy reserves. Yet the hilarious stories can fill a book. More importantly, though, think of the influence you have in forming a future man or woman. Your investment of time and energy toward your toddler's maturity will yield high rewards. To maintain your sanity and sense of humor, it is helpful to understand some typical "whys" in toddler behavior. Keep these ten traits in mind.

1. All toddlers are egocentric; it is all about me, my needs, my wants, and my agenda. Toddlers interpret events in an extremely personal way. For example, a toddler who wants

to leave the house and is stopped by Mom will take this as personal harassment, or he'll see a cake and assume it is for him.

These self-absorbed, naive people want neither to share nor to respect other people's needs. This explains why they grab toys away from playmates. Because of their self-interest, toddlers act in ways that seem offensive. They can scream in rage until their needs are met, bite another child out of anger, or knock down another's block tower. Personal space is not recognized nor respected so toddlers freely touch people and watch others' bathroom behavior. Many misguided adults call these tots "selfish" or "insensitive," an accurate observation, but not a tolerant label. Toddlers are self-seeking because they have not had enough life experience to think beyond their own interests. Don't belittle your toddler by saying he's "being a brat!" Remember, we all emerged from a perfect environment where every need was met. Satisfying our needs in an appropriate way takes years to learn. To empathize—or see from another person's view—is a slow process as well. Because you have a home with a self-seeking person, power struggles between you and him are to be expected. Don't take it personally when he won't share, and don't insist he does. Sometimes it's suitable to let your toddler have a "mine" that no one takes unless he chooses to give. With time and practice, he'll find it easier to let others have "theirs" as he feels respected for keeping his "mine."

2. Toddlers are risk takers, the embodiment of guiltless energy. They climb, ram, throw, jump, touch, run, push, and put everything in their mouth. They resent physical and verbal restraints. Their mighty muscles and new nerve endings need tactile stimulation to properly mature. Yet, these children cannot predict which behavior causes injury

or death. Driven by curiosity and newfound motor skills, a toddler's behavior can astound you.

Tremendous supervision is required with this age. And here's a secret to prevent accidental poisonings: when a toddler grabs a pill—you know he is going to put it in his mouth—quickly cup your hand over his mouth. Rather than attempting to pry the pill from his grip, simply intercept it from going into the mouth.

> Toddlerhood is generally accepted as the period from twelve to thirty-six months.
> Brenda Nixon

3. Talk about movers; they dart from one activity to another. Those who don't understand child development expect tots to sit still during story time. Although this age has an increasing interest in TV and books, they usually sit still for only a few minutes. A toddler's attention span is not fully formed, and he needs an assortment of brief activities. As he moves into his third year, he'll be able to sit still for more detailed books and toys. Attention span is like a muscle: the more it's used the stronger and longer it grows. This is why reading aloud to your toddler is a smart start. Read short, simple picture books with easy story lines.

4. They are the ultimate pretenders, believing in fantasy and the bizarre. These young minds accept that dogs talk, the cow jumped over the moon, and hairy monsters hide under the bed. Illogical thinking is what toddlers do. In this make-believe world, they feel powerful. In the real world, they know they are vulnerable. Respect this susceptible stage by carefully choosing your words. Fantasy gives rise to fears, and a toddler can misinterpret the comfort we try to offer.

5. Toddlers are parallel players; they play alongside agemates, not with them. Watch a group of toddlers and you'll be convinced that they're playing with each other. You hear them copy words, respond to questions, look at their playmate, or

imitate him. This is healthy intellectual development, not playing together. They are actually learning by observing and imitating. They are playing in the group—individually. As toddlers move toward their third birthday, they begin to cooperate in mutual play. You see more sharing of playthings and pretending "house." Around this third year of life, they even seek out same-sex playmates. Then you see the "boys" against the "girls" mentality.

6. They are consummate language learners; words are quickly taking on meaning. However, words are not the primary tool of communication—behavior is. Young toddlers get frustrated with their inability to express words so they throw tantrums, bite, and scream with frustration. By using the few words they recognize, toddlers gather information. They often ask simple, yet multiple questions—"why?" is a favorite. Questions become a way of communication. Lynsey and Laura both drove me crazy with their "why?" Although I was thrilled for their curiosity, there were days I had to say, "Mommy's ears are tired of questions." Honestly, I thought my ears would bleed from overuse.

All toddlers are eager learners, but due to their language limits, they often learn better from experience than from your explanation. Your tot may experiment with words or get meanings mixed up. You might hear "no" when he means "yes." When you talk to your toddler, use simple words and phrases. Usually two- to three-word sentences are right for a one-year-old, while four- to six-word sentences work with the older toddlers. "My child talks in full sentences," you might say. If he's a first-born child in your family, he will probably have amazingly advanced conversation skills. And it's true; girls use more words than boys do.

7. Toddlers can't tell time nor understand time concepts. They're concrete thinkers; something must be visible or

touchable to make sense. In my experience I hear parents frequently say things to toddlers like, "After a while we'll go to Grandma's." If your toddler cannot touch an "after a while" he doesn't have a clue what you mean. *Is it after a while time yet?* he might wonder. Since 80 percent of learning is visual, it's better to give children something to see rather than a time concept. "When I come in your bedroom, it will be time to go" is more meaningful. As a concrete thinker, your toddler lives in the Now. So to gain more of his cooperation when it's time to clean the room, say, "Now we put away toys"—this is both visible and immediate.

8. Toddlers are moral hesitators; the ability to figure out right from wrong is on pause. I hear well-meaning parents claim, "He minds because he knows better!" Child development says, "He minds for fear of reprimand." The capacity to weigh right and wrong isn't in place yet. Your toddler acts without moral reasoning. He refrains from a certain behavior by having learned that he'll get a negative response from you. To a toddler, right is what "gets me approval" while wrong equals "punishment." Around his third birthday, a sense of morality begins. To understand the rightness and wrongness of a behavior is a process. Therefore, to understand ethics like honesty, godliness, loyalty, and integrity requires many years of consistent teaching from ethical parents.

9. They are scribblers; control of each hand and fingers is still developing. Most can't "color inside the lines." It's better to give your tot a pad of blank paper and let him scrawl away. Fat chalk, crayons, and large pencils make it easy for his chubby fingers to grasp. His work does not have to "mean" something. Let him make nonsensical marks. When he proudly shows you his work, the best comment is to describe what he's done: "I see you used green."

10. Toddlers seek independence; their need for autonomy can drive parents crazy. One minute they want your help, the next minute they resist or scream, "Go away!" Most toddlers want to feel independent by putting on their own coat or getting a drink yet they often need your help to accomplish the task. I teasingly remind parents that independence doesn't begin at twelve years but at twelve months. Your best attitude is to be available when you're needed and not when you're not—like a consultant. The ambivalence—of wanting freedom and needing help—is seen in a toddler's emotional extremes. Sometimes he is on an emotional joyride, and the best adult response is to remain seat-belted and stable.

Your toddler needs legitimate limits to feel secure and loved. As he seeks autonomy, give him supervised guidance. He cannot do everything he wants; it isn't healthy, safe, or realistic. But do allow him to do many things for himself so he begins to feel independent. Remember your responsibility and privilege to influence your tot begins with respecting his process of maturity. Along with reasonable expectations based on development, you will enjoy parenting right from the start.

My Success Strategy

Understanding typical toddler traits will help me be a better parent because . . .

break the bottle habit

"That stupid bottle! How do I get her off it at night?" she asked. I looked at the frazzled mom standing before me. "My sixteen-month-old daughter is attached to her bottle at bedtime and hangs on to it during the day too!"

I frequently hear this concern as I speak to parents of toddlers. "The world is a stressful place," I answered. "Most tots need a security item to help calm agitated nerves. Looks like she's using the bottle as hers."

Newborns emerge from the womb with a persistent, forceful sucking skill. This is their principal survival and security source. And one thing that calms a fussy infant is sucking on a breast or bottle or, when that's not available, on a thumb or pacifier. Gradually, as solid foods are introduced, sucking is no longer a survival source. However, sucking on bottles or pacifiers may continue to be their calming behavior. This is when parents can introduce another comfort item such as a soft blanket, stuffed animal, or small toy.

Lynsey attached herself to a cuddly, overstuffed, white lamb given to her as a baby shower gift. "Lambie" became Lynsey's comfort companion. We took him with us to Grandma's and on road trips to ensure Lynsey's unbroken peace of mind. I saw to it our second daughter, Laura, bonded early to a comfort item. Hers was a lime green bunny with long, floppy ears that were perfect for stroking.

Nightly, Laura curled up in her bed, an arm snug around "Bunny" and two fingers gently rubbing his ear until she drifted to sleep. "Lambie" and "Bunny," now threadbare from years of love, are tucked safely in my cedar chest along with other cherished parenting memorabilia.

The bottle, however, must not become this primary security item. Why? There are numerous problems awaiting the toddler with a constant bottle habit.

- She gets full on liquid then does not eat solid foods at mealtime.
- Steady use can interfere with language development.
- Teeth can become misaligned.
- Lying down while sucking on a bottle aggravates ear infections. Liquid may flow through her Eustachian tube into the middle ear.
- Constantly sucking on a milk- or juice-laden bottle can contribute to tooth decay. According to the American Academy of Pediatrics (AAP), "Dental caries is the most common chronic disease affecting children in the United States. It is 5 times more common than asthma and 7 times more common than hay fever."[1]
- It's unsightly to see a healthy toddler running around with a half-empty, stale bottle dangling from her lips.

Enough to convince you? Children should find safety and security in meaningful objects, routines, and people, not from oral gratification. Although some pediatric professionals recommend that tots should not use a bottle after the age of one, don't feel discouraged if yours isn't weaned as soon as she blows out her first birthday candle. The AAP says that it may take up to six months to wean your toddler off a bottle.

Your first step is to replace any milk or juice you're now putting in her bottle with water. That will protect her teeth from the possible rot. Then work on relieving her daytime bottle use. Some parents have found that by insisting the child use the bottle only while seated at the kitchen table, their toddler soon loses interest in it. After all, it's no fun to run to the kitchen and stay confined there just for a bottle fix.

> Provide toddlers with a sippy cup featuring two handles and a snap-on lid with a spout to minimize spills.
>
> Brenda Nixon

You might also try keeping your toddler's mouth "occupied" with conversation or song. Sips of water from a straw or sippy cup can satisfy some need for sucking.

After a week or two off the daytime bottle, progress to nighttime weaning. Typically, the bedtime bottle is the hardest for toddlers to give up.

Observe your daughter during the day to see what familiar toy or blanket she prizes most. Then offer that item to her at night in place of her bottle. She may fuss at the change you're proposing, but your resolve will help her move away from the bottle and connect to another familiar item for relaxation. Avoid being too aggressive or you'll have a power struggle on your hands.

Gently, persistently offer her the same item each evening to replace her bottle. Reassure her with a statement such as, "You can use this now but no more bottle." Encourage her with positive reinforcement. Compliment her efforts and create an environment where she chooses to stop needing her bottle. It may take several nights to get her switched over, but you must be consistent for her own good.

One way to make your toddler feel in control is to use a hands-on approach with a "bottle funeral." Together with your child, throw the bottle in the trash and wave good-bye or bury it in the backyard. This visual closure helps her end bottle dependence.

You are justified and wise in wanting to break this unnecessary, potentially harmful bottle habit now. After all, you don't want to be like the mom who told me, "Andy clung to the nighttime bottle until he was almost two and then replaced it with not one, but *two* pacifiers. That took a little longer to break!"

Be prepared. During times of high anxiety such as a new sibling entering the family, illness, or a pet's death, it's normal for your toddler to want to start the sucking behavior again or become overly attached to her comfort item. However, with your help and her gradual maturity, she'll eventually learn other ways to cope with life's stresses.

My Success Strategy

I understand how important it is to allow my toddler a security item. If she doesn't have one, I'll introduce . . .

help tots obey—the positive way

"Stop throwing that!"

"Don't touch it."

"Quit hitting."

"No running in here!"

Sound familiar? In an effort to discipline, parents tell kids what *not* to do. Trouble is, this stops short of being effective: either they repeat themselves or engage in verbal debates with the kids, or the child continues the behavior but in another form. Negative commands teach kids to end their action but fail to teach the desired one. Little Suzie may stop touching but doesn't know what to do instead. And left to her own imagination, she may come up with another behavior that is equally annoying or inappropriate.

Youngsters—especially toddlers—have immature thinking skills. They lack the complex ability to replace a negative behavior, one that gets them in trouble, with one that's immediately appropriate. So when parents say, "Don't run," a child doesn't know a suitable substitute behavior. I've seen kids try to comply by slowing to a skip, a gallop, or walking rapidly trying not to run. Then the parent yells again, "I told you not to run." Since there was no clear guidance, the child didn't quite know what to do. "Walk" often gets obedience over "No running."

To be fully effective, begin by telling your tot what *to do* in a kind, matter-of-fact tone. In discipline we can be kind and firm. Kindness refers to our tone of voice. Firmness refers to our follow-through. Instead of "Don't take off your shoes" say, "Keep your shoes on." Rather than "Don't stand up" state, "Sit down" and replace "Don't get out of the car!" with "Stay here." Simple and specific.

Prevent ugly confrontations in public in advance by saying "Hold my hand" or "Stay by my side." Before going to another adult's home, make it pleasant and positive by saying, "Play with the toys we brought," or "Ask before you touch anything."

Have you ever served lunch to fifteen famished, frantic preschoolers—that's thirty chubby, exploring hands? When I taught preschool, lunchtime was always interesting. Handing out brown bags and boxed lunches to my class was akin to serving a table full of octopuses. I could have wasted my breath screaming, "Don't grab his sandwich" or "Stop that!" Instead I stated in advance, "Put your hands in your lap" and they did . . . usually. This approach gave them a precise direction they could follow. I saved myself unnecessary words and repetition. As they sat with their hands crumpled in their lap, I was able to quickly deliver their meal. With all the children served, I said, "Now you may eat."

"But," you challenge, "that sounds too controlling," or "I don't want to be bossy." My response? Who is the authority? When denied clear limits, children feel insecure, and then their behavior becomes increasingly bizarre as they search for some guidelines. In the home parents must assume their role as the leader and be in charge, thus giving children a sense of security.

These days many parents are enamored with giving children choices. "Do you want to go play at Brian's house?" may be appropriate but not, "Do you want to put on your seat belt?" When your child doesn't have a choice, he must be given a directive: "Buckle up." When appropriate, he can be given opportunities to choose. However, there are instances when decision-making belongs to you alone, and skillful parents recognize those times. Running full throttle toward a busy street, your tot must hear and obey your command, "Stop!"

> In automobile terms, the child supplies the power but the parents have to do the steering.
>
> Dr. Benjamin Spock

One way to be effective in discipline is to tell your tot what *to do* right from the start.

Chances are he'll obey because he's heard an exact instruction. And fewer negative words make your home a more positive place to live and learn.

My Success Strategy

I want our home to be an affirming environment, but I need to discipline. Today, how can I turn a negative direction into a positive one?

tame temper tantrums

Has your youngster ever thrown a temper tantrum? Mine did in a busy Kansas City mall. Imagine my embarrassment and challenge to discreetly handle Laura's outburst in public.

Every toddler, for whom independence is a passionate issue, will attempt a tantrum. Variation in temperament means that some are more passionate and persistent about it than others. Trouble is, if we don't handle it skillfully, this negative behavior will be reinforced. It becomes a habit or pattern for gaining satisfaction. I know a twelve-year-old boy who still falls on the ground kicking and screaming in protest when something doesn't go his way. Children whose tantrums are tolerated and reinforced are most at risk for emotional problems as adults.

Children will resist, test limits, say no, and try to get their own way. Occasional resistance to you or angrily stomping her foot is *not* a tantrum. Those are normal, difficult behaviors. A tantrum is when your child loses control, perhaps throwing herself on the floor, howling and shaking. You will probably see the first of this behavior between fourteen and twenty-four months of age. The best medicine—ignore it. Do not get excited, talk to her, send her to time-out, or cave in. Go directly to another activity and simply ignore her ugly

> Children whose tantrums are allowed or encouraged are most at risk for emotional problems as adults.
> Brenda Nixon

behavior. At the moment she quiets or calms herself, make a comment on the improved behavior. Something like, "Oh, you've quit crying. Let's read a book now" is sufficient. Exalt your child's self-calming ability. This way you give attention to her amiable, relaxed behavior and redirect attention to a positive behavior. This is skilled parenting.

"What? You mean I don't punish her for the tantrum?" No. Research shows that punishing unwanted behavior is less effective than rewarding the positive behavior you want to see.

Observe your child vigilantly. When you see a meltdown coming, prevent it by altering the surroundings or shift to a quieter activity. Some children throw tantrums as a result of overstimulation.

Caution: if your child is throwing tantrums several times a day, injuring herself, or destroying property, seek professional help. Discuss it with your pediatrician or family counselor. While many tantrums are pure manipulation, some have other underlying causes, which require a different response.

Let's go back to my daughter. I turned away from her public tantrum in the mall. She regained her control. I then talked to her, and we strolled on down the aisle. I had a sense of parental pride . . . until two elderly ladies flanked me and scolded, "You're a mean mother!"

I'd like to hear your tantrum story. Visit my website at www.BrendaNixon.com and tell me how you tamed it.

My Success Strategy

I'm a good parent even when my kid has a meltdown. One way I won't get caught up in her tantrum is . . .

no biting back

"Don't bite!"

Ever say that around your house? Early childhood parents often find themselves in biting situations and wonder how to handle them correctly. I've heard every cure from "bite 'em back" to spraying a tot's mouth with lemon juice. Please don't. Changing your tot's hurtful action is more successful if you respond correctly instead of reacting with a lemon-juice attitude.

Always try to understand the reason behind the biting. Sometimes your toddler bites not to be aggressive or hostile but to ease the pain of teething. Every infant is born with teeth buds just beneath the gum line. During the first year of life, those buds become razor-sharp teeth and begin pushing their way upward. This painful process makes the sufferer irritable. Biting is an instinctual way to sand down the newly erupted teeth.

Often biting incidents happen as sensory exploration—an educator's term for putting stuff in his mouth to learn about it. The mouth is a powerful information organ, and I've seen kids bite chairs, plants, even the dog. My daughter bit a candle! When I foolishly asked why, she profoundly explained, "To see what it's like."

The simple remedy is to offer your tot soothing, slobber-resistant chew toys. Teething rings, a wet washcloth, or a Popsicle are safe ways of relieving aching gums as well as satisfying that urge to "see what it's like."

> Most biting is a phase and, if handled correctly, a time-limited problem.
>
> Brenda Nixon

Immaturity is another reason your tot chomps. He has little experience with his new passionate feelings. When he gets overexcited, jealous, frustrated, or even bored, he may clamp down on the nearest thing—or person. It is not appropriate; it cannot be tolerated; but understand it is the only option he knows to express himself . . . until you teach otherwise.

Help him become "emotionally literate." Talk about feelings during neutral (non-biting) times. For example, during the day you might say, "You're feeling frustrated with that toy" or "You're excited to see Grandma." Use books to help you teach about feelings. There are wonderful books in the parents' section at your public library. Children love to be read to, so read books about happiness, sadness, anger, and loneliness. By doing so, your tot eventually learns that there's a name for his feelings, and over time he'll use words more often than teeth.

The book *No Biting, Horrible Crocodile!* by Jonathan Shipton is a delightful story about a little boy who comes to school dressed as a crocodile. He thinks he must bite his classmates, because crocodiles bite. He quickly discovers that nobody wants to play with him. It's a childlike view of the unpleasant consequences of this behavior.

Whenever you have biting between two children, immediately separate them. Human bites contain more bacteria than most animal injuries. Wash the wound with soap and water; it's your best disinfectant. Apply antibiotic ointment and cover the site with non-sticking Telfa pads. Never use iodine, alcohol, or Merthiolate, which can damage tender tissues; those sting quite a bit, which will intensify a heightened situation. If swelling, redness, or pain persist, contact your pediatrician.

Then turn your attention to the biter. Acknowledge his feelings ("I know you feel angry") and set boundaries ("I will not let you bite"). Then teach what to do instead of biting: hit a pillow, scribble on paper, or come talk to you. These are all healthier alternatives to biting. Children must learn that *feelings* are always allowable but some *expressions* of those feelings are not.

Once when I was speaking on this topic a mom asked, "What do I do when my son gets so excited he bites his younger sister?" First, I explained the overwhelming excitement youngsters often feel when playing with a baby sister or brother. Then I suggested she give him a replacement to biting, like squeezing his teddy bear instead. She tried it. Later she phoned my office to say it worked. Her son now appropriately expressed his energy overload—making Mom and Little Sis happier. Remember, telling your tot "Don't bite" is only half of your job. The other half is educating him on acceptable alternatives to communicate his feelings.

My Success Strategy

Even though I understand the reasons behind biting behaviors, I cannot allow my child to harm others. One way to prevent his biting behavior is . . .

diaper dilemma

The diaper dilemma causes parental stress because people link their child's success with their own parenting proficiency. That may explain why my workshop "No More Diapers" is one of the most requested, second only to discipline.

There is little correlation between your child's triumph and your overall childrearing abilities. But if you're feeling tense on this issue, maybe a condensed version of "No More Diapers" will help you relax.

Somewhere between two and three years of age, most children add toilet learning to their list of achievements. About 82 percent have mastered it by age three. But it is not solely a calendar issue; it is a readiness-to-learn issue. Factors such as birth order, age, temperament, gender, parenting style, and even the season all play a role in your child's readiness. That's why comparing children is unfair, and using age as the only criterion is unreasonable. Your friend may have hers out of diapers by twenty-four months; that does not mean your child is ready—or delayed. Lynsey, my firstborn, did learn around nineteen months, but she has always been advanced. Laura learned after her second birthday. A friend's son learned when he was nearly four years.

You cannot rush your tot into toilet learning any more than you can make a preschooler master quantum physics. Don't be like the young mom I overheard in the store telling her friend that she's teaching her ten-month-old! By the time her child is two this mom will be greatly frustrated, not to mention the child.

> When parents are unable to wait, and they impose toilet training as their idea, the child will feel this as an invasion.
> Dr. T. Berry Brazelton

First and always, watch to see if your child is ready for this complex task. Readiness for toilet learning is a package deal. When she comes to you complaining about being wet or soiled and understands most of the things you say, then you see signs of her language development. When she repeatedly removes clothes, brushes teeth, washes hands, scribbles, walks well, and straddles a riding toy, you have some of the motor (movement) signs. Knowing where the bathroom is located and retelling stories and nursery rhymes shows you cognitive (thinking) skills are progressing. Internal muscles must be developing. You can be assured of this when you notice she remains dry for two hours every day for a couple weeks, and when she constantly wakes up dry from a nap.

An East Coast mom shared, "My husband and my mom were nagging me to get my daughter out of diapers when she was seventeen months old. My head told me that she wasn't ready, but I purchased a potty chair anyway. My husband got fed up with waiting and decided his daughter was going to go on the potty!" She went on to say that it was the biggest battle of wills in their home—with her daughter winning. Months later, she explained, her daughter walked over to the potty, sat down, and did her business.

It is a joyous occasion when you can declare your home diaper free. One parent sent me this email message: "We figure it has been nearly six years with at least one kid (all three for about fifteen months) in diapers. It has taken us over twenty-two thousand diapers at over five thousand dollars, not including wipes and diaper cream, to get past this phase. We are thrilled and proclaiming this good news unto the world!!!" Just wait until your toddler is ready, or toilet teaching can turn into a year-long struggle with feelings of failure.

When the timing is right to promote the potty, remember that your child is just as eager as you are to succeed at this grown-up task.

My Success Strategy

In toilet teaching I need to practice more . . .

a toilet teaching hurdle

He's almost three years old. He pees in the potty but does not release his bowel movements. Recently he started holding them in, became constipated, and now is on a prescription laxative. His parents are frantic. They feel they're running out of sources to help and report having nightmares over their son's condition and when he'll be trained to use the potty completely.

This scenario is real. Most parents spend a massive amount of time, energy, money, frustration, and discussion on the issue. And it explains why toilet teaching has become one of the leading reasons behind reported child abuse.

According to a review published in *Pediatrics,* about 20 percent of developmentally normal toddlers will refuse stool toilet training at some point between eighteen and thirty months of age.[1] This nearly three-year-old's behavior had become unhealthy, though. The fact that the problem had spiraled to constipation suggests three possible root causes: a power struggle in the home, poor nutrition, or physical problems.

When a child senses Mom or Dad's pressure to perform, he will often dig in his heels. One way to take a stance on independence and control at the toilet is to withhold. Learning to use the toilet is a complicated skill, so parents are astute to be relaxed, gently consistent, and patient with their child.

To avoid making your home a pressure cooker, design a pleasant potty time by reading a book to your toddler or singing songs together. Some parents find it helpful to have special "potty toys" for this occasion. Make the statement "It's time to go to the potty" rather than ask your toddler, "Do you want to go?" Making this statement may appear as if you're controlling your tot, when in truth you're structuring the situation with a reminder. Your child is learning to control her own toileting behavior, but she needs your help through frequent reminders. This is one success tip on my *Finally, No More Diapers* CD, available through my website, www.BrendaNixon.com.

> Bowel and bladder training has become the most obviously disturbing item of child training . . . in our society.
>
> Dr. Erik Erickson

Be sure to compliment him every time he sits on the potty, even if he doesn't "deliver." Never force your child with, "Sit there until you do something!"

Also, if your child goes to daycare or is in a group care setting, allow him to watch peers participating in toilet use. This will boost his interest and desire to learn.

Poor nutrition can complicate digestion and trigger hard stools. You can avoid this by insuring your toddler receives high-fiber foods. Fruits, vegetables, and other high-fiber sources along with a reduction of dairy products will help his stools to be soft. Regular bowel movements will then be easier.

Sometimes a physical impairment causes elimination problems. An acute illness can also make your toddler suffer from hard stools. Then he avoids the discomfort of straining by simply holding it in. It's always reassuring to have your child seen by a pediatrician for a physical and neurological evaluation when you experience long-term toileting problems. Chronic constipation accounts for five percent of pediatric primary care visits.

The clinical community (physicians, pediatric nurses, child psychologists, and others) grants that no one theory or method can address every toilet teaching problem. However, your individual pediatrician, who usually knows you and your family situation, can effectively guide you during this process. You can also find valuable toileting resources at the end of this book.

My Success Strategy

To learn all I can about appropriate toilet teaching I will . . .

"i shoulda listened"

Have you ever asked your kid the same question over and over again? Smart parents know the value of listening when their child answers, but sometimes we're distracted. A mom shared this story with me as her gentle reminder to pay attention when kids talk.

> I hoisted ten-month-old Susan up on my hip, grabbed my three-year-old son, Matt, by the hand, and squeezed into the crowded restaurant. Our day was a flurry of errands and appointments when, around noon, Matt whined, "I'm hungry!" So I found a nearby fast food place for a quick bite in between activities.
>
> The long wait in line was agonizing. Finally our order arrived. I grabbed the food tray with my free hand and shuffled Matt, Susan, and myself around to an empty table. The aroma of steamy hamburgers and fresh French fries filled the air.
>
> Plopping Matt's food on the table in front of him, I positioned Susan in a booster chair. I tightened the straps around her chubby thighs and turned to question Matt, "Do you have to go to the potty?"
>
> "No," he answered, reaching out for his sandwich.
>
> I slumped down in a plastic chair and pulled myself to the table. With a sigh of relief I opened the paper that surrounded

my hamburger, picked it up, and lifted it to my lips. Just as I opened my mouth for that first warm bite I sniffed something nasty. A quick scan around the room revealed nothing unusual. But the foul whiff hit me again.

> You must keep a sense of humor during the twos and threes in order to preserve your own sanity.
>
> Dr. James Dobson

Now Matt had problems with potty training so I feared the worst. *Oh no, that kid's had an accident and I don't have any clean clothes with me.*

"Matt, do you have to go potty?" I asked.

"No, Mommy," he answered as I wiped off Susan's face.

"You hafta go potty, Matt?" I repeated.

"No."

Susan began squirming in her chair. I snatched her hamburger just as her elbow knocked it off the table. Then that horrible odor hit me again.

"Matt, do you have to go potty?" I repeated, knowing I hadn't truly listened the first time.

"Nope."

So I bent over and discreetly looked in Susan's diaper. It was clean. By now I was convinced my son was lying to me.

"Matt, I smell something. Did you have an accident?"

"No!" he insisted, but my doubtful glare caught his attention.

In the next moment you could've heard a pin drop. The restaurant froze and everyone silently stared at us because, with a smirk across my young son's face and eager to prove me wrong, Matt jumped up from his chair and yanked down his pants. He bent over and loudly announced, "See, Mom, it's just gas!"

My Success Strategy

Next time my little one says something to me I will . . .

to spank or not?

Spanking is a furiously debated issue and one that may begin for you in these early years. Parents, both for and against the practice, herald research and quote childrearing experts who support their position. I've met parents who are militant in their stance and condemn others for opposing views.

As a speaker, I've been criticized by a few audience members because I didn't tell parents to spank as an act of love and godly parenting. Some Christian parents claim the Bible commands them to spank, while others believe less physical methods are equally loving and appropriate. Research is confusing; advice is conflicting. Who and what does a parent believe?

One reason people argue for spanking is that it is seen as an acceptable way to teach children not to do things, to stop them when they're being annoying, and to encourage them to behave in appropriate ways. It's been documented that the southern United States practices spanking more than other areas, and some cultures do it more than others do. Obviously, just as there's no one right way to raise a child, there's no one right way to correct a child. I came to my own decision regarding this discipline method, and you must too.

There's a little information from both sides of the argument presented here. Maybe this will drive your curiosity to research the issue and make a decision you can live with.

In *The First Three Years of Life*, researcher and author Burton L. White, PhD, asserts, "There is no evidence that children who have been spanked (*not* abused) when they are young become either aggressive older children or abusive parents."[1] The long-term research needed to test that theory, says White, hasn't been done. Psychologist and author of *The Strong-Willed Child*, Dr. James Dobson, agrees. He says it is nonsense that "specialists" claim spanking makes kids more violent and teaches them to hit others. White says, "Two-thirds of the successful families we have observed from all levels of society have used occasional mild physical punishment with their children after they entered the second year."[2] Yet, both caution parents on the use of spanking. Dobson recommends reserving this response for a child's "willful defiance."

Our children are as good as gold,
And always do as they are told;
Psychology we've used for years,
Then, too, we've spanked their little rears.

Unknown

In May 1995, *Parents* magazine published a persuasive article, "What's Wrong with Spanking?" The writer referred to Benjamin Franklin's famous line "Spare the rod, spoil the child" as a "mentality," declaring her uneasiness with spanking. She could not "in good conscience endorse it as a loving and caring discipline method."[3]

Several years ago, the American Medical Association (AMA) released a study by Murray Straus, PhD, codirector of the Family Research Laboratory, University of New

Hampshire, Durham. Depending on how you read his study, you can come to different conclusions.

Dr. Straus suggests that if parents reduce or eliminate spanking it "could have major benefits for children and reduce anti-social behavior in the society."[4]

However, he admits that frequent spanking doesn't necessarily lead to anti-social behavior; that would be like saying that frequent smoking always leads to death from a smoking-related disease. Dr. Straus concludes with, "Corporal punishment is associated with an increased probability of societal violence," but "even if all parents stopped hitting their children, it would not mean the end of violence."[5] So agrees Dr. Sal Severe, author of *How to Behave So Your Children Will, Too!* He devotes chapter 18 to enabling the parent to "evaluate the practice of spanking," but cautions its use. To read more, check out "The Debate over Spanking" published online at the Clearinghouse on Early Childhood and Parenting, http://ceep.crc.uiuc.edu/eecearchive/digests/1997/ramsbu97.html.

If you choose to spank your child, first stop and ask yourself three questions: Is it safe? Is it effective? Is it safer and more effective than alternatives? These questions can be your criteria before employing any course of discipline. Harshly used, any form (time-out, consequences, verbal reprimands, etc.) of discipline when you're angry and uncontrolled can inject painful emotional wounds and cultivate bitterness in your child.

Occasionally, I spanked a young Lynsey and Laura. Those times occurred when words were ineffective, or when I needed them to immediately stop a dangerous behavior. However, I've learned, through twenty-six years of parenting and research, that while spanking halts one behavior, it does not bring about the desired one. It's my job to teach appropriate behaviors, not just stop inappropriate ones.

Thus, the controversy continues to exist. So what do you do? To me, the squabble over spanking is really about a method, not the *need* for discipline. Kids need to accept that the adult is in charge and to learn self-controlled, respectful behaviors. Moreover, they feel loved when parents take the time to patiently and persistently discipline. So discipline your child, and refrain from criticizing others for their child-rearing practices.

The real issue becomes what you are doing to continually teach your child self-controlled, respectful behavior. It takes a great deal of forethought, patience, and time to discipline. It takes stamina to learn what works with your child. The one thing experts do agree on is that parenting demands enormous perseverance.

Whatever your method, remember this: anyone can discipline your child without loving him, but you cannot love your child without disciplining him.

Isn't parenting complicated?

My Success Strategy

Discipline is teaching my child how to behave whether or not I use spanking. My plan for teaching appropriate behavior involves . . .

clinging toddlers

I was speaking to a group of mothers about separation anxiety. One audience member raised her hand and told me about her nineteen-month-old. She explained that her toddler suddenly wanted to be held more than ever. He was clinging to her, following her around the house, and screaming when she walked out of a room. It was about to drive her nuts. She worried, "Is this *still* separation anxiety?"

While this behavior appears similar, it is not separation anxiety. You've seen it: a baby cries for his departing parent at the daycare, church nursery, or baby-sitter's home. Separation anxiety, an emotional and brief phase, begins at around eight months. But this mother's description of her toddler tells me the clinging phase is happening. A toddler's rapid strides in self-discovery and independence, around sixteen to eighteen months, collide with his dependence on a parent. Most toddlers become confident, if not arrogant, chattering, making choices, and handling toys. However, they still need a parent for refuge and identity.

Sound confusing? It is to your toddler too. The reassuring news: you don't do anything to make your toddler cling. Stay-at-home moms don't cause or perpetuate this. Contrary to some parents' fear, picking up your toddler and holding him does not cause or perpetuate this. The clingy phase is just that: a time-limited, outward sign of a toddler's phase of inner conflict. He wants desperately to grow up and away from you, yet he still needs you for safety and security.

> If we allow our children to be dependent when they are young, they will become happily independent as they mature.
>
> Dr. Brenda Hunter

What to do? Be tolerant; do not ignore your tot nor demand he stop. Allow the clinging. Be available, but go on about your business. If necessary, give a brief hug or say something soothing like, "I'm here and you are safe." Your relaxed attitude will eventually help your child overcome his clinginess.

I have a photo of me doing dishes with Lynsey hanging on my leg quite contentedly. She was around eighteen months old and just needed the refuge of Mom's leg for a while. I'm glad I kept the picture as a token of her toddler ambiguity. Soon after the picture was taken, Lynsey felt secure enough to release her grip and pursue other interests.

Research shows that the more available and reassuring you are during this brief phase, the better. Psychologist and author Brenda Hunter explains, "If we allow our children to be dependent when they are young, they will become happily independent as they mature."[1] In other words, let your toddler cling, and he will ultimately cling less.

Sometimes I wish Lynsey, now a twenty-six-year-old RN, had wanted a reassuring bear hug. Happily, though, her self-confidence and independence have led her to new horizons. I wouldn't want it any other way.

My Success Strategy

When my toddler clings to me I need to . . .

cabin fever relievers

Is your child bored and bickering with you? During long, gray winter months or on rainy days your child may suffer a fever . . . cabin fever. You know the symptoms: feeling isolated, trapped, restless, and easily agitated. She feels like screaming—maybe you do too—and she craves a change of scenery. It's an unpleasant "fever" everyone struggles to avoid. To relieve your tot, try these fun, inexpensive, and easy ideas, which will also help her development.

Grab a blanket and a book! Get cozy with your tot in a chair or by the fireplace. Kids of all ages love hearing stories and the sound of your voice, and these young years are especially impressionable. The undivided time your child shares with you brings a feeling of comfort that will be connected with literature. With books, you can meet new people, visit faraway places, or travel through time with your tot. Books also build your child's language and concentration skills.

Play games! Two-year-olds love to play hide-and-seek and chase games. Three-year-olds can begin board games such as Candyland and Chutes and Ladders. Games teach kids how to take turns, how to practice patience, and how to lose or win gracefully. Reinforce academics such as colors, shapes, and counting during fun, playful games. Card games such as Old Maid strengthen your tot's small hand and finger muscles. Your older child can play Yahtzee, chess, and checkers.

Ignite imagination! Young children love dressing up and pretending. Offer your tot a basket with old clothing, hats, shoes, large costume jewelry, etc., and it may be just the nudge needed for self-entertainment.

> Children are at their most difficult halfway between birthdays—at two-and-a-half, three-and-a-half, and so on.
>
> Dr. Michael LaCombe

Create artwork! Use crayons, markers, paper, chalk, and chalkboard to get those artistic juices flowing. For toddlers, avoid coloring books and demands to "color inside the lines." Instead encourage imaginative drawings. Phrases like "Tell me about your picture" and "You are using red to color" build your tot's self-esteem. Be sure to display that fantastic Picasso on the refrigerator at your tot's eye level.

Produce playdough! This simple recipe requires little time and can really beat boredom. First gather two cups flour, one cup salt, one tablespoon alum, two cups boiling water, two tablespoons oil, food coloring, and fragrance oil (the last two are optional). Next, mix together the flour, salt, and alum. Carefully stir in the boiling water, and if using, a few drops each of the food coloring and fragrance oil. If you invite your child to use a spoon to stir this mixture, you must give constant supervision. Add two tablespoons oil. Mix dough together and, when cool to the touch, knead until smooth. The warm, soft dough is therapeutic to frazzled nerves and strengthens a youngster's fine motor skills. Store in an airtight container and this playdough will remain soft and usable for months.

Cut up with catalogs! Use old mail-order catalogs or magazines to cut out pictures of people, pets, trees, etc. To develop cognitive (thinking) skills, encourage your child to search for pictures of the same color, season, etc. Your little one needs practice at using scissors because it builds strong hand muscles. Be sure to supervise, though, or you may have newly designed curtains.

Plan play groups! One way to model hospitality is to plan visits to other people's homes or to invite a playmate to your home for short visits. Remember, toddlers need lots of supervision and duplicates of toys to avoid fighting. Children older than three years can play together with a little less competition, but stay close by in case you are needed as a peacemaker.

Assemble an obstacle course! Kids and empty boxes go together. Place some large empty boxes around the floor for your child to crawl in, on, and through. Add more obstacles like a chair, step stool, soft pillows, large laundry baskets, etc. This is a terrific activity for using stored energy, motor skills, and imagination.

Make music! Kids make noise, so channel it. Make instruments for a marching band. Drums can be made from empty oatmeal boxes, coffee cans, or a pot and wooden spoon. Cymbals can be created from lids of different-sized pots or pans. Cover one side of a block with coarse sandpaper and rub two papered blocks together for sand blocks. Rhythm sticks can be made from two empty paper towel rolls or old newspaper rolled up and secured with masking tape. Now get out the kazoo. Research says that making music is one way to stimulate your tot's brain development for future math skills.

Build blocks! Bag blocks can be made by filling large grocery bags with crumpled newspaper. Stuff each bag full, fold over the open end of the bag, and tape it shut. Make several bag blocks—the more the better. These are fun for jumping or sitting on, tossing, and rolling. Older children can help younger siblings make the bag blocks. You've just recycled, and your tot has made inexpensive toys.

Pretend ocean play! Fill your bathtub with blue water (add a few drops of blue food coloring), throw in floating toys, and watch your child's imagination take off. No, the food coloring does not turn your little munchkin into a blue genie, nor does it stain the tub. Since kids love water, maybe you can persuade your little one to take off her clothes and jump in. This is a sneaky way to get 'em clean. When my girls were toddlers and I wanted them to take a bath, there would often be an argument. To avoid the debate, I diverted their attention with, "Do you want your water pink or blue?"

Imitate animals! Take turns mimicking an animal sound and then guess which animal it is. Your tot might say, "Moo." "Hmm," you say puzzled, "That can't be a cat or a turtle. I know—you're a cow!" Your tot's memory skills and imagination will be stimulated as you imitate animals.

Begin an indoor yard! It's never too early to teach a basic agriculture lesson. Place a sponge in a glass dish. Pour in just enough water to half fill the dish. Sprinkle on grass seeds and push each gently into the sponge only until wet; don't immerse the seeds under water. Keep the sponge moist, watering from the bottom as needed. In a few weeks, you and your child will have a small green yard, which you can "mow" with safety scissors.

Magnify mysteries! Nurture your child's sense of wonder. Use a plastic magnifying glass to discover and explore details of familiar objects. Your tot can examine her hands, toes, a bottle cap, your pet's hair, a piece of newsprint, a leaf, and much more.

Snow memories! If there's snow, go outdoors and build a snowman, woman, child, or castle. Look for animal tracks;

play follow the leader; create angels or other shapes. Inner tubes, boxes, or trays make good sleds for youngsters. All family members can help clear snow from sidewalks or cars. You also might shovel away snow for an older or sick neighbor. Tell your tot that the greatest North American snowstorm in history happened in February 1959 when more than fifteen feet of snow fell at Mt. Shasta Ski Bowl, California. Now, capture these memories with your camera. Then go indoors for a warm cup of cocoa, a snuggle, and a good book. Since the season of parenting is so short, make a photo album or scrapbook of your frolics in the snow.

Combat boredom by always making sure toys and books are in low places where your tot can easily reach them without coming to you for assistance. This builds her independence and self-esteem.

If your child is playing quietly, or at least contentedly, don't interrupt. I practice the "if it ain't broke, don't fix it" philosophy in parenting. But when cabin fever does get to your child, remember it's only temporary. Be prepared to offer a couple of activities, giving your child freedom to choose.

Just as you gain confidence through knowledge and experience, so does your child. With the new ideas you suggest, your child learns ways to self-entertain. With practice, she becomes more confident in her initiative and abilities.

When your child is older, come back and read this chapter again to refresh your cabin fever strategy. Best wishes for sunny and safe days ahead.

My Success Strategy

To keep myself and my child sane, my plan of action for cabin fever is . . .

outdoor safety to save a life

Kids love warm weather and spending time outdoors. But never assume your child recognizes those dangers lurking outside. Instead, develop the habit of practicing safety precautions to insure fun in the sun without resulting injury. Here are a few tips:

- When loading everyone in the car, feel car seats and buckles first to know how hot they are. The sun can heat a car's interior to a scorching 140 degrees, and that's enough to burn tender skin. Many parents store beach towels in the car to throw over hot seats.
- Prevent painful sunburn by using an SPF (sun protection factor) 15 sunscreen, even on cloudy days. Sunscreen products labeled "broad-spectrum" protect against UVA and UVB radiation. An SPF 15 blocks out 93 percent of the burning UV rays. For maximum effectiveness, apply sunscreen twenty to thirty minutes before going outside. Do not use sunscreen on your newborn (zero to six weeks); rather, protect him from direct sunlight with a bonnet or cap, sunglasses, and lightweight cotton clothing. Reapply sunscreen

about every two hours. If your toddler swims or heavily perspires, reapply sunscreen. Remember too that sunscreen usually rubs off when you towel your tot dry. As you plan your outdoor activities, keep in mind the sun's rays are strongest—and most damaging—between 10:00 a.m. and 3:00 p.m. Often, parents do everything known, but their tot still burns. Sunburn symptoms typically reach their peak within forty-eight hours. If your tot experiences the red, hot, and painful symptoms, a thirty-minute lukewarm bath with one cup of baking soda is soothing to the sunburned skin.

> Skunks, raccoons, bats, and foxes carry rabies. Squirrels sometimes do. Chipmunks, rabbits, mice, and rats do not.
>
> Dr. Michael LaCombe

- Try to use sunglasses on your child that block UV rays. The UV protection comes from an invisible chemical applied to the lenses, not from the color or darkness of the lenses. Look for an ANSI label.
- Take along cool water and offer your tot frequent drink breaks. Water is especially important because it rehydrates body cells. One symptom of dehydration is fatigue. Avoid beverages with sugar and caffeine, which do not truly quench thirst.
- Safety-proof wherever kids might play—your yard, driveway, garage, parks, and even Grandma's house. Since babies and toddlers are extremely curious, speedy, clueless about danger, and put everything in their mouths, you have the right mix for a fatal accident. Before I let my children even play in the sand I checked for sticks, glass, broken toys, or droppings from friendly critters.
- Always be on guard when your child is around contained water sources. Toddlers are top heavy so they

easily fall headfirst into pools, fountains, and buckets. When they can't maneuver their head out to breathe, even an inch of water will be deadly—within five minutes. I think it's terrific when a little tyke helps Dad "wash" the car, but Dad must put the bucket of water up high and keep a close eye on his precious tot.

- Look for rusted nuts, bolts, screws, cracks, or rotted wood on playground equipment. Each year about two hundred thousand children go to hospital emergency rooms for playground-equipment-related injuries. Also, take along antibiotic cream for minor skin abrasions. Watch for the open S-style hooks that can scratch or snag clothes. On your child's attire, remove strings from hoods and around the waist to prevent catching on equipment and possible strangulation.
- Most children eventually plead, "Can I have sparklers?" And many adults add these to their arsenal of summer fireworks, thinking, *What's the harm?* The harm is, these little sticks of colored sparks heat to 1,800 degrees, melt nylon clothing (I know from experience), and cause severe burns. More than five thousand children under fourteen years are injured every year by fireworks. Prevent regrets by enjoying professionally run fireworks displays and forgo shooting them off at home . . . where most accidents happen.
- Dogs are kid magnets. When we walk in the park with our miniature dachshunds, Andy and Opie, kids run to bravely pet them. Usually I stop the youngster with, "Ask if you can pet the dogs," even though I know mine welcome attention. Never assume that the pet is safe. Teach your tot to ask pet owners before touching their animal and not to stare at a dog. Dogs take eye-to-eye contact, especially from children, as a challenge

and may bite. Also, keep in mind that intact male dogs are more aggressive than their neutered counterparts. Every year children suffer injuries from dogs that "look cute."

Nearly all youngsters, with their adventurous spirit, have no thought for safety. With their boundless energy they go carefree from one activity to another. These precautionary tips will reduce accidents as you and your tot make fun, happy memories in the great outdoors.

My Success Strategy

To protect my child from outdoor dangers, I need to . . .

the binky blues

"Our two-and-a-half-year-old son has had a 'binky' since infancy," one mom wrote. "He had gotten to the place where he hardly would go without it. The other day he was throwing a major tantrum about taking a nap. In frustration, he flung the binky across the room. Like a good little dog, I retrieved it, only to have him fling it again and scream, 'No binky!' Since Mommy was at the end of her rope, I hastily replied, 'Oh, what a bummer, no more binky' and took it away permanently. My question is, Was this cold turkey thing too much?"

Mom had a handful of woes: her son's tantrum about naptime, his dependency on a pacifier, her exhaustion, and her guilt over going "cold turkey." As I replied to her question, I tried to focus only on the binky issue, although others added to the situation. My initial response was, "A two-and-a-half-year-old still wanting a pacifier is not a monstrous problem. Constantly demanding it is."

It's a problem when, as with anything, it's overused. Steadily sucking on a pacifier can prohibit language progress. And dentists suggest it can affect the incoming teeth. Also, when a tot has only one means of self-comfort, that may suggest a socialization problem. Pediatrician and author Dr. T. Berry Brazelton has a good rule of thumb. He advises removing the pacifier when it has become a habit and a tool for manipulating parents.

To help you avoid a meltdown like this parent experienced, here are some prevention tips. You've heard the old saying, "Prevention is the best cure." Likewise, in parenting, you can evade many problems by not starting them.

> If you've never been hated by your child, you've never been a parent.
>
> Bette Davis

In the beginning, make pacifiers available only when trying to calm a distressed infant or for naps and nighttime. When a toddler can hardly go without it, that suggests to me he was given it all day, every day.

Another prevention tip is to provide additional comfort items like a stuffed animal or cozy blanket. Help your tot rely on items in addition to a pacifier. Lynsey slept with "Lambie" until . . . well, she'd be embarrassed if I told. It was a familiar bedroom security object to compliment her pacifier. To our delight, Lynsey gave up her pacifier long before she surrendered "Lambie." Laura attached herself to "Bunny." His long, floppy ears are threadbare from years of being stroked as Laura eased herself to sleep. But her pacifier lost its charm around her second birthday.

There are conflicting opinions on how long tots should use pacifiers. Personally, I see no harm in bedtime use for up to three years. If she is using it only to fall asleep and to soothe herself, then she's using it to a good end. However, Dr. Burton L. White, author of *The First Three Years of Life*, considers pacifiers acceptable only to seven months. Dr. Brazelton says that parents should take it away after the first birthday.

This two-year-old's tantrum was a complicated issue. I wanted to assure Mom that normal toddlers *are* negative and independent and resist naps. His behavior, although obnoxious, was not uncommon, but it caused her emotional exhaustion, which impaired her skills and desired outcome. As parents, we do not need to get emotionally entangled with our children. A statement like, "I know you don't want to take a nap and it's time to lie down," is a way of acknowledging your child's feelings without absorbing them. As prevention for future binky tantrums I suggested she lay her tot in bed, hand him the pacifier, and walk out. If he throws it across the room, he goes without. Don't give him further response.

Now to her question, "Was this cold turkey thing too much?" Yes. It added fuel to the fire. But the deed was done. Even though I rarely advocate "cold turkey" solutions when working with children, my answer to her was, "Forge ahead!" The binky demand had become a tool for manipulation. I suggested she stick with her decision to confiscate binky. Children need dependable parents who keep their word.

"We have not given it to him since," she later wrote. Although unpopular, her perseverance paid off. "He laid in bed today," she said, "looked at books, and whispered to himself for about an hour. Finally he fell asleep . . . without binky."

My Success Strategy

When I want to break my child from the pacifier I will . . .

feeding finicky toddlers

Got a toddler who's shy about new foods? Are you struggling to get your young one to eat nutritious meals? Testy toddlers can have timid taste buds. And by the time they're two, *no* is a favorite word. One study shows that boys tend to be fussier than girls about new foods.

Avoid stressing out about feeding your toddler. Keep mealtimes social and relaxed. If your tot refuses something, don't force, cajole, or say, "Sit there till you eat it!" These negative stigmas on eating make meals a battleground with food as the weapon and can usher in eating disorders.

Many well-intentioned parents make the mistake of running back to the kitchen for a different dish if their child turns up his nose. The better way to handle this situation is to prepare and serve tiny portions frequently along with favorite foods. Just the familiarity of the rejected food makes it less intimidating and more enticing to a toddler's curiosity. It can take up to fifteen tries for a child to accept the new food. However, when he samples something of his own accord, chances are he'll be open to trying other new foods.

Also, be a good role model. Sit with your toddler and nibble new foods yourself. As your tot watches you, he's gently nudged to try new dishes. Start early in offering food variety; it's easier to get a one-year-old than a two-year-old to try a strange dish. By the time I was seventeen, it was too late for me to sample the new dish Grandma prepared—cow's tongue.

The Baby Bistro Cookbook by Joohee Muromcew advises parents not to cook a separate meal for their tot; rather give him "a dumbed-down" version—for instance, a less spicy one—of what the parents are eating. Packed with 150 kid-tested recipes, *The Baby Bistro Cookbook* offers directions for preparing an entire week's supply of dishes and pediatrician-approved information on adapting recipes to suit your tot's age and tastes.

My family loves blueberries. In the summer, we pick them to store away for winter months. Some summers we go in June for the bountiful early berries and again in August for the smaller, but sweeter, late ones. Some years it's only possible to pick once.

Blueberries are high in fiber and iron, low in fat, and packed with Vitamin A and C because their dark coloring absorbs the sun's rays. They are one of my favorite fruits to cook with because there's hardly any prep time involved.

How did I get my kids to try this funny little fruit? Two ways: repeated, family-fun experience and trying new recipes. At the farm, I picked up recipe sheets and chatted with other like-minded connoisseurs. I learned to make refreshing blueberry lemonade, jam, and scrumptious blue-goose pie.

One summer, I experimented with a thick and creamy energy drink to start our mornings. The first time, I used lemon yogurt, which gave an interesting contrast to the blueberries. My kids sampled and loved it, requesting the shake again. The second time, I tried nonfat blueberry yogurt to give it a more intense flavor. They loved this version as well. Either way they frequently begged me to make "the milkshake" for breakfast. It was the perfect on-the-go drink when we were running late.

Once you try it then you too can test variations. I've found that plain nonfat yogurt can be substituted for the flavored ones. Sometimes I slip in a tablespoon of wheat germ to boost the fiber content. However, the wheat germ gives the shake a bit of a granular texture and makes it harder to clean the blender.

> Being a picky eater is part of what it means to be a toddler.
>
> Dr. William Sears

Here's my low-fat, high-fiber, colorful, lip-smacking nutrition drink for breakfast. When you serve it, your tot may think you're silly, but you know you're sensible. He may gulp it down without realizing its benefits. Then you can smile with smug delight.

Blueberry Milkshake

8-ounce container nonfat yogurt (lemon or blueberry)
½ cup frozen blueberries
1 teaspoon vanilla
Honey to taste (optional)

Combine ingredients in a blender and whirl until smooth. Pour into a glass and bon appetit.

My Success Strategy

My job is to prepare nutritious food and serve it creatively. How, when, or if my toddler eats is his job. I will relax about eating situations by . . .

3 parenting your preschooler

the power of play

"He's not learning a thing!"

What's play good for? Some parents fear their preschooler will not "learn" anything if he just plays. But the contrary is true. There are multiple reasons you want to encourage periods of free, unstructured, uninterrupted play in your home. Play is:

Useful for emotional stability. A three- or four-year-old who is fearful of a situation can express his feelings through playful actions rather than words. Pretending to be in an imaginary situation or an animal gives him opportunity to try out different solutions to his fears. A pillowcase can become his superhero cape and make him fearless, or the empty toilet paper roll can be his police megaphone.

Psychologists at Yale University Dorothy and Jerome Singer have devoted their lives to the subject of children's play. They summarize their observations of children in free play:

> We have found that those who engage in make-believe, what Piaget calls symbolic play, are more joyful, and smile and laugh more often than those who seem to be at odds with

themselves—the children who wander aimlessly around the nursery school or daycare center looking for something to do, who play in a preservative way with a few blocks, or who annoy their peers by teasing them or interrupting their games.[1]

A way to calm. Unstructured play is an outlet in which youngsters can express strong physical drives. The body is growing, and play gives opportunity for physical mobility and muscle control. Often the boundless energy your preschooler has needs to be released through active play. Research shows that children who are allowed to play often are less likely to be aggressive and hostile.

> Play is often talked about as if it were a relief from serious learning. But for children play is serious learning.
>
> Fred Rogers, *Mr. Roger's Neighborhood*

A vital source of learning. Problem-solving approaches, language, and cognitive and emotional skills are supported through free play. Children learn more easily when they're actively involved rather than passively absorbing an adult's lecture. Play helps fine motor skills such as eye-hand coordination—a critical precursor to reading and writing skills. Preschoolers whose play includes make-believe have more advanced language skills than kids of equal intelligence and perform better in intellectual reasoning tasks.

The Yale research also showed that kids who engage in make-believe are better "sharers" with children and less demanding of parents and other adults.

Create a playful atmosphere with age-appropriate toys that are within his reach. You don't have to have all the latest gadgets or software. Give him old cooking utensils or empty boxes. Make sure there are a variety of playthings so his play can vary from simple to complex. I used to rotate the toys my daughters played with. That way they didn't get bored with the same things.

You can value your child's play too. When he's building with blocks or driving a car through a shoe box converted to a garage, say something like, "I like the way you're working." Play is his work. When you respond this way, you encourage him to take pride in his play and motivate him to play more.

Next time adults doubt your child is learning because he's "just playing," you can enlighten them with the benefits of play. Or use the words of the late Mr. Rogers: "Play gives children a chance to practice what they are learning. . . . They have to play with what they know . . . in order to find out more, and then they can use what they learn in new forms of play."[2]

My Success Strategy

A hectic, structured schedule is not helpful to my child. Rather, I'm being a good parent to allow some free play and will begin . . .

monsters in the closet

"Good night," I whispered to my three-year-old Laura. Pulling the sheets up and tucking them beneath her chin, I tiptoed out of the bedroom.

"Night, Mommy," her young, high-pitched voice echoed.

Moments later as I was walking through our hallway past her room I noticed her closet door was open. Quietly I slipped in and closed it.

Later, I walked past her room and noticed the closet door was open again. For an instant I stared into her darkened bedroom, confused. Positive I had closed that closet door, I wondered, *Am I in the Twilight Zone?* Then, for the second time I softly slipped in and closed the door.

A third time, I walked past Laura's bedroom. That closet door was open! "All right, what's going on here?" I objected. "Laura, are you opening your closet door?"

"I hafta let the monsters outta the closet."

Well, at least I wasn't going crazy. Rather, in Laura's immature mind there were monsters hiding in her closet. Her active imagination was preventing her from resting. But, with as much wisdom as a three-year-old can muster, she reasoned that if she let them out then she could sleep.

Her thinking did not surprise me; that we were already in this stage of development did. I knew preschoolers had unruly imaginations—they confused fact and fantasy. I just wasn't ready for Laura to be at this point so soon.

> Childhood is frequently a solemn business for those inside it.
>
> George F. Will

Not wanting to debate or criticize her thinking, I thought of a way to relieve her fear. In my most motherly voice, I ordered, "You monsters get out of here so Laura can go to sleep!" When they were gone, because I checked, the door was shut. Then I reassured Laura that all were gone so she could go to sleep.

Rather than argue with a preschooler's imagination, it's usually best to acknowledge her fear and reassure her that you understand. Many parents have found that Monster Spray—aka water—works well to chase off scary inventions of the mind. Some argue that you shouldn't reinforce a child's fantasy—that you should make her see the facts. Ever try reasoning with a pooped preschooler at bedtime who insists there are monsters in her closet?

This stage of development has its upside and downside. On the upside, preschoolers play alone for longer periods than when they were toddlers. They can spend hours "varooming" with trucks, serving a tea party, or being the "teacher." Some preschoolers with vigorous imaginations invent pretend friends. That in itself is healthy. But it's usually the pretend friend who knocks over the plant and gets dirt on your carpet. On the downside, preschoolers often tell stories that sound larger than life and have more frequent nightmares.

This brief time in a parent's life can be the perfect opportunity to practice understanding and give comfort. Since an action adventure stimulates an already lively imagination, limited TV viewing keeps bad dreams to a minimum. And following regular bedtime routines calms your youngster, which lessens imaginary monsters. As a preschooler ages she will realize that her monsters or imaginary friends have gone away. She'll be better at knowing fact from fiction.

Before going to bed that night, I peeked into Laura's room. The closet door was closed and so were her eyes.

My Success Strategy

To prevent some bedtime monsters I will . . .

choosing the right preschool

Thirty years ago, preschool was a luxury for children of affluent parents. Kindergarten was the first school experience for the rest of us. Neither I, my siblings, nor our friends attended preschools. The closest we came to academics before age five were Sunday church and Vacation Bible School.

The tide is swiftly changing for several reasons. Today, working parents need the additional childcare a preschool offers. Putting their child in preschool is defined by some as good parenting; a few fear their child will be left behind peers; and many parents presume three- to five-year-olds require an academic shove.

Don't subscribe to the modern myth that preschool is imperative. Raising a happy, healthy, curious child does not happen because of an organized program—it happens because of you. Rather than pushing your child to "perform," letting him learn at his own pace will give him the greater advantage.

Should you choose to send your child, avoid a preschool that makes academics its main focus. In her book *Mothering,* pediatrician and child psychiatrist Dr. Grace Ketterman cautions, "Do not practice, and do not allow, any major emphasis on academics until kindergarten."[1] She cites that new research is showing that kids are getting "burned out" before kindergarten.

Nonetheless, enrollment in early childhood programs, both public and private, has grown from four million in 1970 to presently over six million. Whether you use preschool by necessity or by choice, the suggestions here will help you determine the right one.

First, be finicky and start early asking many questions. By beginning your search months before your child needs preschool, you will have time to do a more thorough search. Your parental legwork will give you added confidence when later dropping off your darling.

Next, don't be seduced into a false security that a preschool with a waiting list is superior. With today's high demand for childcare, most preschools have a long waiting list.

Always select a program that reinforces your family ideals and values. Do you want a religious preschool, a corporate-run one, or a neighborhood program? Do you seek traditional or Montessori curriculum?

Consider your child's temperament. Do you have a self-starter or one who needs a push and constant supervision? Do you have a child who thrives on structure or one who is spontaneous? How does your child adapt to change? Does your child successfully separate from you? Answer these questions, then seek a preschool that matches your child's disposition.

To ensure a minimum level of health and safety standards is met, seek a licensed preschool. Licensing does not influence curriculum, so a licensed church preschool still has freedom to teach religion. As an added bonus, try to find a preschool that is both licensed and accredited. Accreditation—which isn't required by state law—is offered to early childhood programs through professional organizations, such as the National Association for the Education of Young Children (NAEYC). An accredited program tells you it meets high standards.

Ask to read the prospective preschool's written philosophy, curriculum, and goals. The NAEYC, for instance, encourages schools to have these statements written and available to parents.

> The important thing is not so much that every child should be taught, as that every child should be given the wish to learn.
>
> John Lubbock

Check out class size. The NAEYC recommends no more than ten three- or four-year-olds to one adult and twenty as a maximum group size for this age. Avoid programs with overcrowded rooms. I know a Kansas City preschool that crams as many preschoolers as possible into one room, which overburdens the teacher. And when the teacher is stressed she passes that on to the children.

Ask about opportunities for staff continuing education. Professional growth is important in any occupation and, I feel, especially so in caring for our future leaders. At least one teacher should hold an early childhood degree. But that's not a reason to send or withhold your child. Academic letters behind a name do not guarantee teachers are childcare savvy.

Visit a preschool at least twice during the hours your child would attend. Take note of the teachers' attitudes and interactions with the children. Ask yourself: Are teachers friendly, firm yet gentle, and consistent in discipline? Are they giving attention to a crying child? Or respecting the child who wants privacy? Do they kneel down to each child's level? Do teachers allow for uniqueness or do they work at making cookie-cutter kids?

Teaching an energetic group of three- and four-year-olds is enormously exhausting. I know from experience.

Preschool—and all—teachers need support, respect, and parental participation. Good preschool teachers appear to love their job, are attuned to the children, and have quick responses. Ask yourself: *are these the people I would want to be left with all day?*

Look for a rich literary environment: plenty of age-appropriate books easily accessible to the children. Beware of preschools that insist children sit down and read in a formal way. It's possible for some three-year-olds to read, but children of this age benefit more from being read to. They need opportunities to make up stories, engage in dramatic play, and talk about ideas. Do you see a play kitchen and dress-up areas where children can use their imaginations and role-play?

Scan the room where your child will be playing and spending most of his time. Is it bright, cheery, and child-proofed? Think about the environment in which you'd want to spend your day. Do you see children's artwork hung at their eye level, or is it displayed only to impress visiting adults? Does the artwork reflect creativity and individuality? Forget about any prospective preschool that displays cloned artwork.

A sand and water table, paints, musical instruments, clay, and other manipulatives acquaint children with the arts and improve eye-hand coordination. Do you see some of these available? Is the play area attractive and inviting to a youngster? Do you think it encourages exploration? Remember a child's work *is* play; they learn valuable lessons even when it appears they are just being amused.

Since children learn by moving around, ask how often the children play outdoors, have opportunity to run, and play without an adult making all the rules. This gives children a chance to use their large muscles, interact with peers, and learn social behaviors. Recess and free exploration are also ways to decrease a child's adrenaline—a stress hormone.

Finally, consider the director's attitude and relationship with both teachers and children. The director's attitude spreads through a preschool like wildfire. Is this person warm yet professional, sensitive and caring, willing to chip in and help out? Do teachers stay at the preschool or is there constant turnover?

A stern-looking director dressed as if she (or he) works in an executive suite, rather than with energetic preschoolers, is hardly embracing this profession. My favorite, and one of the best, preschool director is an older woman who wears casual clothing and daily sits on the floor with her kids. They are drawn to her. She loves them; teachers know it, parents know it, and most importantly the kids know it.

My Success Strategy

If I don't send my child to preschool, what am I going to do to support his continued development?

raise responsible kids

"Everyone should have kids. They are the greatest joy in the world. But they are also terrorists," said comedian Ray Romano.[1] You can relate if you're the parent of a three- to five-year-old.

The preschool years are packed with pandemonium, loud voices, sassy talk, and oodles of activity. It's hard to corral a child long enough to teach him anything, especially responsibility. But this is the age it must begin. Did you know responsible children are more pleasant to be around, are successful in school, and grow up to be productive, conscientious adults?

If you're the parent of a busy preschooler, teaching responsibility requires repeated lessons because it's a value that takes time and patience for your child to absorb. Right now, begin your lesson by teaching him to help himself.

You taught your tot to bathe and brush his teeth, right? Now, demonstrate for your preschooler how to make his bed. Next, have him join you and do it together. Then expect it to be done each morning. Avoid redoing the job if it doesn't suit you. Instead, compliment his effort and you'll see progress.

When my girls were around age three, I taught them both to make their bed. It was one way I tried to help them learn self-directed care of their own possessions. Did they always do it perfectly? No. But it taught them duty, increased their self-esteem, and helped them feel in control of their property. It also eased my workload.

> Never help a child with a task at which he feels he can succeed.
>
> Maria Montessori

A child needs a "job" in the family. Involve your preschooler in household chores. Prepare him now in small ways to take on responsibility. Then he won't be shaken in later years to find that part of living includes some giving.

Teach your child self-help skills, which include preparing breakfast cereal, warming a toaster pastry, getting his drink, and putting away dishes. First, do these activities with your child before expecting him to do them solo. Your kitchen may be a mess, but your preschooler will improve with regular practice and your recognition. The payoff comes on those rare mornings when you sleep late. You won't be disturbed with, "I'm hungry. When ya gonna get up an' fix breakfast?"

Responsible people also care for their own clothes. Picking up clothes can be first taught by making it a game. "Race the Clock" is a fun challenge to get every item picked up within a certain time limit. Or try picking up clothes together as you and your preschooler sing a song. "Pick up your clothes," I said to Laura. Later I walked into her bedroom, and the floor was spotless. *What a great kid,* I thought. But a quick check under the bed and on the closet floor revealed a pile of clothes that had been previously scattered about the room. I'm not sure if, in her young mind, she thought she'd picked up her clothes or if she was good at sneakiness. Show your preschooler where dirty clothes belong—not under the bed or stuffed behind the dresser.

Often parents sabotage their own efforts to teach responsibility. Does this scenario sound familiar: you go in your youngster's room, cringe at the sight, and in a nanosecond you tell yourself you can't stand it and pick up the mess? All the while, you're nagging and complaining, "Why do you make such a mess?" Your child stands watching you clean up his clutter. He quickly learns he's not accountable for the job because you do it for him. Deborah McClellan, MS, of the University of Illinois Extension, writes, "Researchers have found children as young as 18 months offer to help with household tasks. When parents made a simple statement such as 'Just look at those papers' toddlers would respond by picking things up. The key was leaving the task undone—so the child had the opportunity to do it. The amount of work performed is linked to the amount parents leave for children to do."[2] The "offers" of help usually become less frequent as they get older, so start teaching now.

When your preschooler forgets his obligation—and surely he will—resist rescuing. Let there be nothing clean for him to wear. Remember, sometimes it's not strong-willed kids but weak-willed parents who create problems. Your home is a microcosm of real life. After months of reminding Lynsey about her dirty, nasty clothes, I got smart and put a laundry basket in her room as a visual reminder of what to do with dirty clothes. That stopped my nagging and gave her opportunity to learn self-care. Later, when she was around eleven years, I taught Lynsey how to sort and wash a load of her dirty clothes. As a teen, she was completely responsible for her laundry. I learned that when my behavior changed, my daughter's behavior changed—for the better.

The road to responsibility is long. As your preschooler becomes more skilled and independent, increase his household tasks. Remind him to bring home notes from his teacher—or return your notes to her. Encourage him to get up and dressed on time and compliment him when he does. Teach him to pack his school lunch. With a little instruction, preschoolers are able to select wholesome food, wrap it properly, and pack their lunch. Not only does this free up your time, but it allows your child to feel successfully independent and nurtures self-esteem. "My parents treated me like I had a brain—which, in turn, caused me to have one," said Diane Lane. To demonstrate that work comes before play, foster the habit of chores first. Children can earn privileges by showing they are dependable and reliable.

Always remember, your child can't learn to be responsible unless you give him responsibilities and he sees you acting responsibly. Are you being accountable for your words and behavior? Writer and civil rights activist James Baldwin keenly observed, "Children have never been very good at listening to their elders, but they have never failed to imitate them."[3]

Teaching your child responsibility right from the start gives him a sense of self-reliance and confidence. Kids who are accountable in the home have a big advantage in the classroom, and when mature can meet life's challenges as a responsible, productive adult.

My Success Strategy

Letting my child help and have responsibility is letting him feel needed, important, and independent. A job I can give him is . . .

talk less, act more

One crisp, fall morning Laura, my five-year-old, was dressing for school . . . supposedly. Instead I found her half-naked, staring in the closet and mumbling to herself. Somehow she managed to find numerous distractions to prevent progress. "Laura, get dressed!" I urged for the umpteenth time. But to my chagrin this sweet kindergartner continued dawdling. "Laura, are you dressed yet?" I asked again.

"Aaahhh!"—as Cathy in the Hallmark comic strip exclaims—I discovered I was nagging my kid. At this point in life, I'd been parenting a total of twelve years; I should've been smart enough to prevent this behavior. Laura was not doing what she was told, and it was partly *my* fault.

How did I correct the situation? Logical consequence. I wanted to teach my daughter that *she* was acceptable even though her dawdling *behavior* was not. I marched into her bedroom and calmly, firmly—and finally—announced, "Laura, if you aren't dressed when your bus comes, you'll have to finish on the bus." Wide-eyed, my daughter gazed at me with a challenging smirk on her face. I walked from her room and neither mentioned it again nor checked in on her.

Several minutes later I heard the squeal of bus brakes followed by the familiar horn toot. This was Laura's signal to dart out the door and onto the bus. Anxiously I bit my lip wondering if she was clad. To my surprise and pleasure Laura was—except for socks and shoes. Calmly I said, "I'll put your socks and shoes in this sack so you can finish dressing on the bus." Then I handed her the sack with the remaining clothes. Laura stared at me with disbelief and gaping mouth.

My barefoot daughter and I shuffled down our driveway toward the waiting yellow bus. Slowly Laura mounted the steps, toting her bag of unfinished business. She meandered through the aisle and sat down on a seat. "Have a good day. Love you," I cheerfully reminded as the doors closed. Then I watched her bus drive out of sight . . . feeling a bit shameful.

> If you want children to keep their feet on the ground, put some responsibility on their shoulders.
>
> Abigail Van Buren

Did I wonder if I did the correct thing? Yes. Did it bring success? Yes. The next morning, without a reminder, Laura was fully dressed *before* her bus arrived. What did my logical consequence teach her? Lots: time management, self-discipline or ownership of behavior, and the knowledge that Mom can be trusted—she means what she says.

Fortunately, this logical consequence was necessary only once. I share my minor triumph to help you effectively discipline through consequences.

Most children learn from experience rather than passively absorbing words (reprimands or nagging) from adults. Consequences also give kids opportunity to make choices about their behavior. And, thankfully, it saves us words because we talk less and act more.

For maximum effect any consequence must be:

closely related to the misbehavior
allowed to happen (no rescuing)

In my situation the grueling part was allowing the consequence to take place. It would've been easier to plop my little darling on the bed and hurriedly pull on her socks and shoes. But she needed to learn self-direction, and, as her teacher, I wanted the consequence to guide her future behavior. Logical consequences permit children to learn from reality.

Every day there are opportunities to use logical consequences to manage your child's behavior. For example, to help your tot stop throwing food on the floor you can state, "When you throw food on the floor you have to pick it up" or for the budding artist who scribbled on the wall, "Here's a rag, now wipe it off." Children soon learn that all behavior has outcomes. When you forewarn and then allow consequences to happen you send a valuable message: "You live by your choices." Hopefully, your child will begin to make better and healthier choices.

Regardless of your child's age you can allow her to experience the consequence of her choice. Laura's older sister had been taught to do her own laundry. Like anyone who fails to wash dirty clothes, Lynsey soon learned when she didn't do laundry she had "nothing to wear to school!" Some parents have told me that they removed the door to their teenager's bedroom as a consequence of repeatedly slamming it. One mother who was tired of nagging "Brush your teeth" told her son he'd help pay for the cost of his cavity.

Natural consequences are also an effective teaching tool. As adults we've learned that leaving our house on a rainy day without an umbrella will get us wet, or that working all day without meals makes us hungry and grumpy. Within reason—and safety—allow natural consequences to happen in child discipline. Rather than cajoling or getting into food wars with kids, simply state, "If you don't eat, you'll get hungry." Let nature take its course without a snack rescue.

When your child complains shortly afterward that she's hungry, say, "I know you must be hungry; you can eat when we have dinner."

Roberta saved herself a battle of words. She allowed natural consequences to teach her three-year-old. Nathan, anxious to play with the neighborhood kids, begged to join his pals out in the snow. "Wear your coat, Nathan," Roberta advised. Like many rambunctious preschoolers Nathan was oblivious to his mother's guidance and dashed outdoors. Shrugging her shoulders Roberta confidently said, "When he gets cold he'll put on a coat." Within minutes of her prediction, a shivering Nathan ran in the house, looking for something to wear. Roberta handed him the coat without a scolding or "I told you so" but with a little motherly smugness.

You can use positive outcomes to motivate your child. At times, I told a young Lynsey, "If you stay right beside my cart, then you may walk in the grocery store." When Lynsey was older, her positive outcome included, "When you clean your room, you may go play with your friends."

Be patient: some children need repeated encounters with a consequence to internalize the rule. This type of discipline may take time to be effective in your home. Be persistent: when you give in, it indicates a lack of respect for yourself. Say what you mean and mean what you say. Then your child learns to trust you. He learns that your love is unconditional while your acceptance of his behavior is not.

My Success Strategy

To make consequences more effective in our home, I will . . .

nightmares vs. night terrors

Parents often tell me about their child's awful nightmare, and then ask what to do. Sometimes I hear descriptions distinguishing it as a night terror. The two are similar. But the handling of each must be different.

Nightmares are scary, outrageous fantasies that wake up a child. They usually happen in the second half of the night when dreams are most intense. Even young babies have nightmares. Preschoolers are the most prone, however, because of their burgeoning imagination. You know your youngster has had a nightmare when he wakes up crying, frightened, or agitated and has difficulty falling back asleep.

To curb nightmares, restrict extra stimulation like TV action adventures or rough-housing with Dad just before lights out. Follow calming bedtime routines every night—children thrive on routine. Then expect your young one to take several minutes to relax into slumber. He cannot turn off his energy like you do a car's ignition.

When your child wakes up from a "bad dream," be calm and understanding. No preschooler, regardless of how good his sleep routines, grows up without occasional resistance to bedtime, sporadic sleepless nights, or a scary nightmare for no apparent reason. Yelling at him to go back to sleep can make things worse. However, saying things like, "I know you feel afraid, but I'm here and it's all right," acknowledges his angst while providing reassurance. It's helpful to identify with him by saying, "Sometimes my dreams are scary too."

Encourage your child to talk about the dream as a way of relieving his anxiety. Avoid statements like, "That's nothing to cry about," or, "Forget it!" which disrespect his true feelings. Many nightmares inexplicably disappear by grade school age.

> Parents must be flexible in order to change their approach to their child when indicated.
>
> Dr. Grace H. Ketterman

Although he feels anxious, and it's tempting for you, resist the urge to take him in bed with you. This may start a habit that's difficult to break. With your assistance, and opportunities, your child will learn to calm himself and cope with fearful situations. Now that's a life skill you want to teach.

Night terrors usually happen shortly after tots fall asleep. They increase in the preschool years and mysteriously decrease after age six. When one occurs, your child may spring up out of bed, rush around the room, scream, shake, breathe heavily, and gaze at you (now that's scary). Believe it or not, he is still asleep. Attempts to restrain him may prove futile; at times a child will shove the parent away. The episode, which occurs in deep sleep, can last from one to forty-five minutes. Some parents put locks on doors and windows if their child is prone to bizarre terror behaviors.

These episodes often follow a stressful or turbulent day. That's why soothing bedtime rituals are strategic parenting. During your routine encourage dialogue about the day to relieve your child of stress. Your best efforts may prevent night terrors, but if one occurs anyhow, here's what to do.

Remain calm and gently redirect him back to bed. Attempts to talk to or awaken him may disturb the sleep cycle. Once he's back in bed, you go back to yours.

One parent wrote, "My son had night terrors. . . . They were bizarre for me and my husband to experience." She explained that her son "was oblivious to them and soon outgrew them."

Your child will outgrow most sleep problems by second grade. If not, or if he experiences an increased frequency, consult your pediatrician, who may recommend a sleep expert.

Laura was five when she had her one and only night terror. I was lying in bed, dozing off to sleep, when a bloodcurdling scream came from her room. Before I could jump out of my bed, Laura was sprinting up and down the hall, arms flailing, eyes wide open. I wasn't familiar with terrors then, and my thoughts raced from her being bitten by a rat to having a seizure. My husband and I corralled Laura and gently guided her back to bed. She returned to sleep rapidly. It was very frightening—for me.

The next morning I mentioned her "bad dream," and she knew nothing. This is the hallmark of a night terror—your child will not remember it. You always will.

My Success Strategy

The difference between a nightmare and a night terror is . . .

what children really need

If ever there was a time for parents to embrace their sacred and enormous task, that time is now. Changes in our society, our neighborhoods, and our families—as well as increasing demands from a rapid-paced, information-rich world—have made the career of parenting more challenging (and important) than ever.

All children are born with basic needs that must be satisfied in order to grow up emotionally and spiritually healthy. One father asked, "How do I know when I'm being a good dad and when I'm not?" The only sure way is to watch your child. Good parenting does not mean a lot of money or tons of toys or team sports. Neither does it demand you have academic letters after your name. Good parenting is perceiving and attempting to meet your child's fundamental needs. Some of these are:

Attention . . . the kind that only nurturing adults, more importantly, the parents, can fulfill. Every person, regardless of age, shares the need to be recognized and the need to belong. Your child's need for attention is real, a basic part of her survival instinct. Regardless of your monetary, academic, cultural, or ethnic background, you have a valuable treasure to give your child: attention.

In the first year of parenting you shared your treasure by responding quickly and consistently to your infant's cries. "Babies cry to announce their hunger or other discomforts and rely on the world, the adults nearby, to correct the problem," explains Elaine M. Gibson, MA. "When we meet a baby's physical needs, we recognize the existence of the child. A baby whose needs are ignored eventually gives up and 'ceases to exist.' In extreme cases of neglect, such infants stop crying when they are hungry and literally starve to death."[1] Remember, to the world you may be one person, but to one person you are the world.

As a toddler, she needed consistent, constructive guidance in how to behave and how to gain attention in appropriate ways. You touched, hugged, and held her. Doing so gave her emotional insurance for the difficult times in life. "We eliminate a lot of problems if we pay attention to our children. I know it is work. No one tells prospective parents just how much time this will take. It is a real responsibility of parenthood. There are no short-cuts," says Gibson.[2]

During these preschool years, continue to play with her, have family meals, maintain predictable routines, and offer specific encouragement for her progress. The simplest happenings outlined in love become a pattern for her quilt of memories. As children age, the need for demand touch—diaper changes or dressing and bathing—decreases, so be diligent about touching in other positive ways. Continue meeting her need for attention through your words and actions. Preschoolers perceive attention from adults as evidence that they belong—in the family, school, or community. Most children believe if they don't get attention, they don't belong.

While she can get attention from grandparents, friends, neighbors, or teachers, never take an "attention vacation" but watch her in public places and when you're in other people's home. Someone once said that love is *doing*, not *feeling*; therefore, love takes time. Convey your love by knowing where your preschooler is going, what she's wearing, and who is supervising her. Get to know those who influence her: friends, teachers, TV characters, and celebrities. Look into your child's eyes when she talks to you.

> Two little girls were discussing their families. "Why does your grandma read the Bible so much?" asked one. Replied the other, "I think she's cramming for her finals."
>
> Unknown

This is not an overindulging attention that makes children crave the spotlight. This is the type that says, "My child is my responsibility—all the time." It takes determination, energy, and some inconvenience to give this parental treasure.

Time . . . to ripen. In our technologically rich society, we expect rapid results, quick answers, and speedy progress. "Microwaves have made us impatient," declares my mother. Children must not be rushed through childhood. They are not microwavable products. Instead, they need generous amounts of time to be who they are—immature and fickle. And we must be patient. Henry David Thoreau said, "Nothing can be more useful to you than a determination not to be hurried."[3] This determination can apply to giving your child needed time to think and invent, relax, pretend, look within, and learn about herself and life.

When given time to relax and play, children develop the art of fantasizing. When older, they become good learners who are enabled to cope with disappointment better than those who have never learned—or lost—the art. Yet highly scheduled, busy days and lives rob children of the necessary time to develop their imaginations.

Make time and give it to your child. Plan unscheduled hours each week for your child to play alone, catch up on chores, unwind, or just hang out with you—no goals. You are not a court jester whose job is to entertain. Now and then, help her learn that it's OK to be bored by having "nothing to do." Tell yourself that it is *good* parenting to give your child what she needs—not just what she wants. And she needs some downtime.

Faith . . . It's difficult to raise good kids in a world that can be difficult or even dangerous. Rather than regarding life as meaningless, give your child spiritual optimism. Teach her to believe and trust in our good Creator. Believe you are divinely guided to this book for information and inspiration. You are on this earth in this place at this time in history to parent this child—you are on purpose. Your child needs to believe that life is sacred, there is purpose, and she is "on purpose" too.

A little girl once confided, "I don't ever feel alone since I found out about God." What a comfort to her that there is a faithful, kind, just Father who loves and wants a relationship with us all.

Recognizing faith as a core component to good mental health and "wholesome development of children," the New York State Youth Commission once published a Children's Bill of Rights stating that children have "the right to the benefits of religious guidance and training."[4] Clinical psychologist and university professor David N. Elkins wrote, "I believe that spirituality is essential to human happiness and mental health." He says that meditation, prayer, rituals, and other spiritual practices have the power to release something in the deepest levels of the human psyche. "Indeed, new evidence shows that religious and spiritual interventions can help when everything else has failed."[5]

From birth to eighteen years, 85 percent of your child's waking, learning hours are spent not in the classroom but in your living room. You are her first and most influential teacher. Decide now what spiritual matters are important to you and teach them to your child. Let your child see your faith in action. Don't just send her to church; go with her and share in an adult activity. Be honest in revealing your moral dilemmas and how you handle them. Natural conversations about faith, bedtime prayers together, grace before meals, and pointing out the beauty of God's creation will make a profound impact on her. The greatest predictor that a child will develop and carry a mature faith into adulthood is simply having regular conversations about faith with her parents.

The celebrated World War II military leader General Douglas MacArthur declared, "It is my hope that my son, when I am gone, will remember me not from the battle, but in the home, repeating with him our simple daily prayer, 'Our Father, who art in Heaven.'"[6]

Now is the time to fully embrace parenting and give your child what she needs. Give her your attention, your time, and a faith for her future. Nelson Mandela said, "We must . . . realize that the time is always ripe to do right."[7]

When children's basic needs are met, they have a greater advantage in life. They can become champions—persons with a sense of worth and dignity, contributors to society, and, if married, faithful and competent mates and parents.

My Success Strategy

I'm being a good parent when I give my child . . .

ready for kindergarten?

Kindergarten is an exciting, anxious milestone for you and your child. And it's only natural to wonder, "Is my child ready?" Even though I am an educator, the mother in me questioned this when our first daughter approached school age. Imagine my surprise—and bruised pride—when early in the school year, Lynsey's teacher told me Lynsey lagged behind in some kindergarten skills.

Wise parents know their child's early classroom experiences shape a lifetime attitude about school and learning. So it's critical that your child is ready for kindergarten and has positive learning experiences.

The word *readiness* means your child's readiness to learn, rather than just knowing some academics or being five years old. Frequently, parents drill their child with numbers, shapes, colors, and printing, assuming this makes their child ready for kindergarten. And, as I share with parents in my toilet teaching presentation, you cannot let a calendar alone tell you when your child is ready for a milestone. Attention must be given to emotional, physical, and social development as well.

Begin early in the spring, watching for the following skills and behaviors. These will help you decide if your child will be ready by the fall.

- Interacts easily with other children, understands the concept of "friend," can name at least one friend.
- Handles crayons, chalk, pencils, scissors properly.
- Performs self-help tasks without assistance, such as dressing/undressing, brushing teeth, preparing cereal, picking up toys and clothes, making her bed.
- Says "please" and "thank you" 50 percent of the time without reminders.
- Can sit still, even for a few minutes (don't count TV-viewing time).
- Listens and follows directions.
- Takes turns, follows rules, plays in a group.
- Knows her and your name, address, age, and telephone number.
- Knows left from right (this requirement differs by school district).
- Speaks in complete sentences and speech is understandable to others not living in your home, such as neighbors, Sunday school teachers, grandparents.
- Asks questions, eager to know, curious.
- Runs, jumps, swings, pedals tricycle, walks on tiptoe, balances on one foot.
- Physically similar in size to others the same age, not unusually small.
- Falls asleep easily and sleeps all night, some nightmares or grumpy mornings are common.
- Generally accepts adult authority; occasional resistance is healthy, while unfailing obedience or overcompliance is not.
- Demonstrates confidence in her own ability to cope with new situations.

- Recognizes numerals one through ten.
- Can take turns.

Remember, size, physical abilities, and emotional development are important reasons to send or withhold her from kindergarten. Be honest in your appraisal of her skills progress and unique personality.

> Education begins at home. You can't blame the school for not putting into your child what you don't put into him. You don't just take your child to ballet class. First, you dance with him when he is a baby.
>
> Geoffrey Holder

Ask your child's preschool or Sunday school teacher what she has observed. Gather as much objective information on your child as possible. Then talk with the school principal, counselor, and kindergarten teacher to get their recommendations. At one school, a kindergarten teacher told me most children come to her printing in all capitals. But her preference is that the children print in upper- and lower-case letters. So she spends the first half of the school year breaking their habit. This is why it's imperative to learn your school district's kindergarten readiness requirements.

Some programs, like Montessori, prefer children write in cursive while others discourage this at the kindergarten level. Get to know your local school district's practices, because there's a wide variety in school districts. At present, there are no national standardized kindergarten criteria.

Doing your homework early in the year can take pressure off any last-minute decision. If you feel your child is ready but lacks a skill, you have the summer to get her ready. Practice with writing and cutting instruments, visit the library frequently, talk to your child about kindergarten, wander around the school building to get familiar with its layout, and make sure immunizations are up-to-date.

Trust your observations and parental instincts. Keep your child's best interests in mind but don't prohibit her from going because of

- your own separation difficulties;
- your neighbors and friends are doing it; or
- you think she can excel in a group of younger children next year.

One teacher said some kids come to kindergarten bigger but still not ready to learn.

If you decide to hold your child back, reassure her that she hasn't failed you or herself. Explain that everyone develops at their own pace and that not going to kindergarten now is the best decision for her. This minimizes competition and teaches her to value her uniqueness.

If you think your child is ready but not five years old yet, contact the school district for early entrance policies. Some schools give testing for early entrance. Others offer a transitional pre-K class.

All educators agree that once you decide your child is ready for kindergarten, get involved. Go to the first open house night, to PTA/PTO meetings, and to the parent/teacher conferences. This sends a message to your child that school is important, and in addition, teachers do form impressions about your interest in your child based on school function attendance.

My Success Strategy

Kindergarten is an important milestone in our lives. To make sure my child is ready to embrace it and to learn, I need to . . .

thumb-sucking sally

A worried mom emailed, "How do I get my five-year-old to stop sucking her thumb?"

"Not an easy answer," I replied.

The developing fetus sucks her thumb. Newborns use their thumb as a healthy self-comforting pattern. Babies who make use of their thumb are easier to live with. Two-thirds of toddlers use a pacifier or fingers. Even an upset preschooler may use the conveniently available digit as a way of soothing herself. Dr. Alan Greene, Princeton graduate and one of the world's most trusted and beloved pediatricians, says, "Between 85 percent and 99 percent of children stop thumb sucking before age five."[1]

So why would the behavior persist into the fifth year? There are many reasons older children engage in this conduct.

Mom's solution hinged on her answers to my questions. First, was the family enduring sudden or chronic stress? Children are perceptive and pick up on the stress in their environment. An onset or increase in thumb sucking may simply be her response to anxiety. If that was the case, I suggested Mom identify and reduce the tension. Then she'd see a reduction in her daughter's unsettling behavior.

Second, was her daughter's behavior only at nap and bedtimes? If so, ease off. I explained that her child was using an appropriate, and transient, way to relax.

Third, I asked if she was worried that her daughter's teeth would be ruined and she'd need braces. I reassured Mom that the occasional thumb in the mouth does not deform upper teeth. According to the American Dental Association, thumb sucking does not cause permanent problems with the teeth or jawline unless kids do it beyond their fifth year. More often, tongue thrust causes problems. Of course, it's always a good idea to talk with a pediatric dentist. He will probably explain that the need for braces has to do with a genetic tendency.

> It is better to be prepared for an opportunity and not have one than to have an opportunity and not be prepared.
>
> Whitney Young Jr.

Finally, I quizzed, "Does it drive you crazy?" If so, the child knows. This is often the big culprit for the habit in older children. When parents feel that thumbs or pacifiers are dirty, wrong, or disgusting, they eventually transfer this feeling to their child. Kids repeat what brings attention. If Mom or Dad nag and coax their child to stop, it only reinforces the behavior. Ignoring it as a brief developmental behavior will keep it that way.

It may be alarming for a parent to see her child curled up on the furniture with a hand protruding from the mouth. Many parents feel this way. About one in five six-year-olds occasionally suck a thumb. Attempting to interfere with what could be a temporary phase causes children as old as eight years to continue the behavior.

Sometimes parents drive this behavior underground with, "I better not catch you sucking your thumb!" Then their child simply hides to do it.

Pediatrician Dr. T. Berry Brazelton urges parents to examine their own feelings about thumb sucking. He maintains that the world is a stressful place for small children. Thumb sucking, Brazelton says, is a healthy sign of competence in self-comforting. I love his casual attitude that very few kids go off to college sucking their thumbs. I even read recently that one percent of adults confess they occasionally do it. Maybe they're the underground bunch.

In parenting there are few predicaments with one easy solution. However, by expecting these situations and planning your strategy beforehand, you will be able to handle it right from the start.

My Success Strategy

Thumb sucking isn't a problem in our home because . . .

bedtime resistance remedy

If you haven't been frazzled by a preschooler who resists going to bed, you're probably not a parent. My younger daughter, Laura, was the Queen of Stall. I defined bedtime as being in bed—with both legs—and lights out. Laura defined it as a time to begin getting ready for going to bed.

And while getting ready, she'd suddenly get an attack of janitoritis and clean her room, neatly fold clothes that had lain under the bed for days, or organize her stuffed animals. Once in bed, she'd jump up with, "I want a drink," or "I forgot to brush my teeth," or the most famous, "I got a *k*ingernail," (fingernail), which one of us would have to clip before she could relax into slumber. My husband or I would holler "Go to bed!" a dozen times every night.

With all my education in child development, the mother in me still fell prey to my daughter's manipulation. I knew in my head that this age dawdles. And I knew preschoolers are great at charming their parents. And I knew they love being in the center of the "action." If an older sibling is watching TV, Dad is working in the garage, or you have company, the three- to five-year-old will find endless reasons to resist separating for bed. But preschoolers need eleven to twelve hours total sleep in a twenty-four-hour cycle. That can include a nap. Half of all preschoolers still need a daily nap. When they are rested they have more energy to grow and learn. So even if my heart said, "Let her stay up," my head said, "Get her in bed and keep her there." Parenting power is knowing something *and* putting it into practice.

> Good mothers need to be tough at times.
>
> Dr. Grace H. Ketterman

What did my husband and I do? Laura loved going to sleep with the hallway light shining into her room. So, we bought a dimmer switch and installed it in her bedroom. Then we explained that instead of the hallway light she could dim the bedroom light to go to sleep. We wanted Laura to sense her ability to sleep alone. So we told her that she could control the level of darkness in her room only if she went to bed on time and stayed there. Then we added, "If you get out of bed we turn off the light."

Of course the first night she had to challenge our word—and the light was turned off. The second night the dimmer switch was lowered once. The third night, Laura went to bed quickly and stayed there. For a long time all we had to remind was, "Stay in bed or I'm turning off the light." We used something important to our daughter so she'd be more committed to changing her behavior.

Dr. Richard Ferber, author of *Solve Your Child's Sleep Problems,* advises closing the bedroom door for a minute. He says that parents can talk through the door to reassure their child.[1] And this method works successfully for many families. Personally, I felt that would have isolated Laura, deepening her resistance to being separated.

Now you might think we ended that very common problem. We did . . . until a couple years later when Laura again jumped up several times at bedtime. It was like she had springs in her legs. Returning to our same strategy, we determined what mattered to her. This time it was money—her independence. We explained that when she stayed in bed, she kept her allowance.

If she got out of bed, she lost a quarter—big money in those days. It was tough to walk in her bedroom early one evening and restate, "Laura, I told you if you got out of bed you'd lose a quarter," then go over to her panda bear bank and shake out the coin. My heart said I was a thief stealing a little girl's money. My head said, "Stick to your word and you'll prevent similar challenges to your authority." My head was right.

Preschool parents frequently tell me similar stories of things they've done to get their kids to bed. And weary parents, at the end of their rope, will try almost anything. I've heard it all, from offering a security blanket or a flashlight to installing a fish aquarium to parents lying about lobsters crawling around the floor. I can almost hear, "Hurry to bed or the lobsters will bite your toes!" One thing is sure, you don't have to get angry to be effective. Instead, remember this three-part remedy for bedtime resistance:

1. Determine what works with your child . . . and milk it.
2. Give her opportunity to gain the independence by sleeping alone.
3. Stick with your household rule.

Today Laura is twenty years old and reasonably skilled at expressing herself. I recently asked her, "Do you remember those nights and why you strongly resisted bedtime?"

"I hated being alone in my bed, especially when I could hear you guys out in the living room having fun without me."

My Success Strategy

At bedtime, I'm in control of myself and the situation. I will make it pleasant and consistent by . . .

sweet dreams—not!

Gritting her teeth, an exasperated mom said, "Susan, my four-year-old, gives me nightmares every night. First, I'll put her to bed and she'll stay. But in the middle of the night, she wakes up and comes to my bedroom. Then, I take her back to hers. She whimpers around that she can't sleep so I end up lying in bed with her, and usually we both fall asleep again. I don't want Susan to be afraid of the dark or feel like I'm abandoning her. But this kid is totally wearing me out, and I'm tired in the mornings. We have to rush around so I can get ready for work and get her to preschool on time. I'm exhausted and sick of this overnight ritual that began a few months ago when she was sick."

In my work with parents, I frequently hear this scenario. First, let me reassure you that in hundreds of homes with preschoolers, overnight battles are being fought. Susan's mom isn't alone in her challenge. If you can relate, help is here. You can conquer this battle in a way that benefits both you and your preschooler.

There are many reasons a preschooler wakes in the middle of the night. With her vivid imagination, she may have trouble staying alone in bed—especially following a frightful nightmare. Nightmares usually occur after midnight or in the wee morning hours. A preschooler's imagination can convince her that a small shadow is a huge monster or a tap on the window is a "bad man" trying to break in.

Another cause behind nighttime waking is medical . . . and gross: pinworms. These little (¼–½ inch long) white worms look like small pieces of thread that cause itching around the anus (without a rash), especially at night. Humans—not animals—are infected with pinworms, and they're extremely contagious. What happens is the adult female pinworm travels to the skin around the anus at night and lays her eggs. If Susan complained "My bottom itches" or her mom noticed Susan frequently scratching down there, Mom would have reason to suspect pinworms and seek medical advice. Pinworms are easily treated with an oral medication. But, because they're so easily transmitted, if Susan had pinworms then everyone in the household (except for tots under two) would be prescribed medication.

However, I diagnosed the underlying cause at the end of Mom's comment: ". . . when she was sick." Aha! When kids are sick, our hearts melt. We want to hold them and make it all better. My guess is, when Susan was sick and unable to get through the night, she'd come to her mom's bed for comfort and attention. Mom probably hugged Susan and escorted her back to her room as a reminder that she must sleep in her own bed. However, like any self-respecting preschooler, Susan would whine that she couldn't go back to sleep. This behavior paid big dividends: sleepy Mom probably climbed in Susan's bed because she couldn't bear to think Susan was afraid of the dark. Remember, though, months prior, Susan wasn't afraid when Mom put her to bed and left the room. If Susan had fears, they would've been expressed as soon as—or shortly after—Mom exited the room. More than likely, Susan enjoyed her mom's comforting bed presence while she was sick. Being exhausted, both of them slipped off into the land of nod. Gradually, Susan learned to depend on her mom to go back to sleep—Mom unwittingly became Susan's overnight crutch.

Childhood illness can become a culprit behind new nighttime problems. When Lynsey was three years old, she was horribly sick with the flu. Her appetite dwindled as her temperature soared, she ached and was lethargic—it was pitiful. Each day, Lynsey moped around, lacking interest in anything. Her typical energetic self vanished. My heart wanted to constantly hold and nurture her. At night, I'd slip into her bedroom, feel her forehead, and insure she wasn't too warm and was safe and easily breathing. It's a Mom thing.

After several days, Lynsey began to respond to the course of medicine and Mom nurture. Her daytime energy returned. But then, at night she started waking up and tossing and turning in her bed. I'd go into Lynsey's darkened room to comfort, calm, and cover her up. I couldn't figure out why she was waking up now at night if she was well. After three or four nights of unexpected interrupted sleep, I told my husband that I was going to watch the clock and see just how long Lynsey remained restless. I knew through some books I'd read that fifteen minutes is usually the longest a child will fuss before drifting back to sleep. Even though in the middle of the night fifteen minutes can seem like an eternity, I was determined to wake myself to watch the time. As usual, Lynsey woke up that night, and I focused on the time. But she kept tossing and turning and crying out for twenty minutes. At that point, I figured something else must be wrong. My mind raced through a course of daily events, back history, and mistakes I may have made with her. Finally, I came up with my best guess: Lynsey was hungry. Since she had recovered from the flu, her appetite had returned. Cautious not to start something new but determined to meet Lynsey's need, I jumped up, grabbed my daughter, and went to the kitchen in the middle of the night. With low lights to avoid unnecessary stimulation, I stirred up a bowl of warm oatmeal. I plunked Lynsey up on the countertop and spoon-fed my hungry daughter. She gobbled up every bite like a famished baby bird. With a hug and an "I love you," I tucked Lynsey back into bed and returned to my own. Silence.

> It can take seven to ten days to conquer bedtime battles with your preschooler.
>
> Brenda Nixon

In the morning, I realized that as Lynsey's appetite returned she was hungry those previous nights. I felt like a jerk for not recognizing it the first time she awoke but was relieved that I figured it out without getting annoyed with her. Fortunately, this one-time oatmeal feed didn't turn into a nighttime problem. But it's given us fond memories.

Often, great parents unintentionally teach their children not-so-great behaviors. What starts out as a benign response evolves into a cancerous lesion. How does a parent *teach* a child to repeatedly get out of bed? By rewarding her with a drink of water, badgering or pleading with her to go back to bed, sleeping with her, letting her get up and watch TV for a while, playing chase games back to bed, or allowing her to go climb into the parent's bed.

Here's a parenting insight: the familiar ritual of a bedtime drink quickly becomes a *learned* need—it's rarely a biological one. For better bedtimes and overnight sleep, parents are wise to not even start bedtime liquids or a snack.

Certainly, any sleep-deprived parent will be pooped. Our bodies cannot take constant sleep interruption without it affecting our mood, behavior, and parenting performance. But interrupting a child's sleep cycle adds to her fatigue as well.

When responding to Susan's mom, I encouraged her, "Honor a consistent bed hour that Susan can't change or manipulate." Mistakenly, parents think kids can make up for lost sleep on the weekend. The idea of making up sleep is a myth; to the body, lost sleep is forever gone. Children need routine and will sleep better when their evenings and bedtimes are comfortably predictable. A regular, comforting sequence of events may prevent problems too.

To end the disruptive overnight ritual, I recommended, "Start by putting Susan to bed with, 'I want you to stay in your bed all night.'" Children need to hear our expectations. The first night, I predicted, Susan would probably practice her habit of waking up and slipping into Mom's bedroom; after all, that's familiar to her. But, "Keep your lights out, get up, escort your darling daughter back to her bed with a calm reassurance like, 'You can sleep in your own bed,' and then leave. Don't climb in bed with your preschooler or worry that you're abandoning her. Once you've gently responded to her—she's assured you're in the house. When she slips back into your bedroom, repeat your behavior, but this time, be mute. Don't add stimulation."

Darkness assists the body in producing melatonin, a sleep hormone. "Each time she comes to your room, quietly escort her back to bed in darkness. Resist your urge to lie down with her, which was her reward for getting out of bed."

When kids have difficulty staying in bed overnight, offer them a comfort item such as a stuffed animal or favorite blanket to sleep with. But they need to learn they have the capability to sleep through the night without the parent's body next to them.

"Eventually," I assured this mom, "you won't have to get out of your bed and escort Susan back to hers. Simply calling out 'I'm here. Go back to sleep' will be sufficient."

Now, I am not against the family bed concept. But most parents tell me they want their child to stay in her own bed, and I want to support their childrearing goal.

Persistence pays. If you want your child to stay in her own bed, teach her that once in bed she stays there. Occasionally parents say, "Brenda, you don't know how strong-willed my kid is!" So? Strong-willed or not, be persistent and insistent with your child. Sometimes I wonder if it's really a strong-willed child or a weak-willed parent.

If overnight sleep issues persist in your home, talk to your pediatrician. Rarely, a child's neurological cycle becomes messed up. Then a sleep professional is needed to resolve the problem before your household has sweet dreams.

My Success Strategy

If my child can't sleep overnight without me, perhaps I'm adding to the problem by sending the message that she is unable to sleep alone. I will make the following change . . .

back to babyhood, what's the problem?

"Brenda, we need to talk," he said to me over the phone. The young father and his wife attended our church and participated in my optional parenting classes, and we'd talked on several occasions about his kids.

"What's the problem?"

"Our five-year-old is acting like a baby. We don't know what's going on."

"How long have you noticed it?"

"About three months now."

We made an appointment for me to visit in their home and discuss their daughter's mysterious behavior.

I sat down at their table with a cup of coffee and both parents across from me looking dismayed. In tandem, they began relating incidences where their kindergartner acted as she did at an earlier age: wanting her blanket, whining, having difficulty sleeping, bed-wetting, talking like a baby, and begging to sleep with her parents. "This isn't like her, Brenda! She's usually pretty cooperative, easy, and independent," they explained.

"Part of being a good parent is being a detective," I said. We don't always know what's troubling our kids and must take the time to find out. The three of us put our heads together to trace back to the onset of their daughter's regressive behavior. I asked a series of questions to stir Mom and Dad's thinking. "Any sudden changes in your family three months ago?"

"No."

"Either of you change jobs?"

"No."

"Moves, new kids, deaths?"

"No."

"Fights at school, bullying, problems on the bus?"

"Nothing we're aware of."

"Hmm," I said. "Something's causing anxiety in your daughter. When there's serious angst, changes in a child's health or behavior occur."

When speaking to audiences about childhood trauma, I explain that kids are like little Martians with their protruding antennae constantly receiving data. Their sensitive antennae zero in on stress in the home and in ways we don't even realize. Absorbing stress and anxiety isn't just a grown-up condition.

Children, especially younger ones, are incapable of verbally communicating their specific needs or fears. Disturbing experiences or abrupt changes such as the loss of a parent or divorce stir up apprehensive emotions that they're inadequately prepared to identify or express. Since she can't say or handle how she's feeling, regression is a common, automatic response. She wants things to again be simple and her life easy.

During times of family moves and schedule upheaval, Lynsey or Laura had developmental regression. At first, the behavior took me by surprise. Then, I was baffled by it.

Sometimes I didn't cope well and yelled at them to "Stop it" or "Act your age." Of course, that was an exercise in futility because it didn't help them, and I later felt guilty. But we're not always attuned to what rocks our kid's world. We need an action plan to discover the cause and respond in a supportive way.

> Rather than simply say she's feeling insecure, scared, or angry, a youngster regresses to a stage that was previously comfortable and familiar to her.
>
> Brenda Nixon

Our look back that day revealed no prolonged illness or injuries, or changes in the family's financial condition, childcare arrangements, or pets. Finally, Dad piped up, "The only thing I can think of happened about three months ago. Our best friends divorced. Their daughter plays at our house. I wonder if she said something about divorce or did something to our daughter to express her anxiety."

"Now we may be making headway," I replied. After a few more suggestions about other stressful events, this was the only thing they could pinpoint.

It is hard for children to accept divorce because of their security needs and optimistic views on two-parent homes. Children at this age have imagined powers and immature thinking. They may think they caused Dad and Mom to split. They may spend time worrying if they are the problem and feel helpless and guilty. They lack logic, so behavior, then, is a form of communication. "Through her behavior, your daughter is saying, 'That's too complex for me' or 'I'm afraid you might break up too.'"

No single response eases a child from anxiety back to age-appropriate behavior. What I suggested for these parents was a three-pronged approach: maintain a consistent household routine, reassure their daughter that their marriage was intact, and during play times give her opportunity to vent her emotions.

A stable routine helps a child feel her world is predictable. Maintain the same meals and bedtimes so she knows her house is a sanctuary. Routine also means all the same rules apply. Just because a child is regressing doesn't mean that discipline takes a vacation. Parents still need to be firm and consistent in their expectations and discipline methods.

Since youngsters may not recognize or have the ability to verbalize fears, it's helpful for parents to "reach behind the behavior" with reassuring comments. Something like "Daddy loves Mommy" or "We're staying married" casually dropped throughout the day is picked up by those childhood antennae. During morning preparations for school, for example, Dad could make a casual comment such as, "I'm glad Mommy and I are married." Even though it's not a direct statement to their daughter, she hears it. I encouraged the parents to also show physical affection in their daughter's presence.

Use calm, relaxed play times to help her express emotions. It's during play times that kids are more open and willing to talk about what's troubling them. I suggested the parents sit together at the table with playdough or a coloring book and gently encourage their daughter to spill the beans. Play has many developmental benefits, but it's also a therapeutic opportunity to relieve stress and baby behavior. During the play time, the parents could also sell their daughter on the benefits of being a "big girl." They could mention that babies can't ride bikes, play with playdough, or go to school.

Both parents agreed to my multi-approach to resolving their daughter's fear. Once her anxiety about divorce subsided, I predicted an improvement in behavior. We planned to meet and talk about it a couple weeks later. But, within a week, Dad saw me at church and said, "I want to give you a report. We tried what you suggested. Then we also added a 'thankfulness' time to our family dinner. We'd go around the table and take turns sharing what we were thankful for. That gave me opportunity to remind all my kids that I was thankful for them."

"How are things coming along?"

"Great! Everything is back to normal . . . well, except for the typical kid behaviors. Our daughter is herself again."

Fortunately, these parents had an issue that was quickly resolved. To some degree, all children will experience periods of temporary regression throughout their lifetimes. If your child displays extreme behavior changes, she continues to regress, or the problem gets out of control, talk to her pediatrician about it and seek psychological or specialized help.

My Success Strategy

At times, my child may return to baby-like behavior. When this happens, my best strategy is . . .

guiding kids through grief

Fatal accidents, terrorist attacks, old age, war, and terminal illnesses are a part of life today. Death is never an *if*: it's a *when* issue. And with death comes stinging sadness over the loss.

Educating children about death and guiding them through grief is something we prefer to avoid, but it's one of our teachable moments. And sadness is more bearable when it's shared.

When it's your turn to guide your child through grief, remember preschoolers grieve differently than adults. Some don't appear sad when hearing that a person died. Helping a child begins with an understanding about how preschoolers mourn. This age:

- will sense a generalized loss. They pick up nonverbal grieving from you, family members, and friends but usually imitate the grief you express.
- doesn't understand death as being final. Because they can't grasp what permanence means, they think dead people continue to eat, drink, and go to the bathroom in heaven.

- has wild imaginations. They may think they're responsible for the death of a loved one, or that if they walk on the person's grave, he feels it, or that if they wish hard enough, they can make dead people live.

And because of their immaturity, preschoolers may express:

- increased dependency on or clinging to you
- increased or intense tantrums
- bed-wetting or constipation
- nightmares

When a death touches your family, here's what you can do.

- Use the words *death* or *dead*; never say "went to sleep" or "passed away." Get used to saying the word so it becomes familiar and less upsetting. Make it clear the dead will not come back, but that they are feeling no pain.
- Answer questions in short sentences using simple, frank words. Avoid answering with lots of details as this may confuse your child.
- Give physical hugs and touch as needed. Loss can leave your child feeling in danger and helpless.
- Explain that being naughty or wishing something doesn't make bad things happen.
- Stick to day and nighttime schedules including the same bed hour every night.
- Dolls or pictures can help you answer questions or explain what happened.
- Let your child see you sad and tearful. He will learn it's OK to laugh and to cry—and that tears aren't forever.

- Read books about grief to your child. Some suggested titles are in the appendix of this book.

To be in your child's happy memories tomorrow, you must be in his life today!
Brenda Nixon

Grieving is unique and personal to children as well as adults. Reach out for help in guiding; utilize your community, church, family, and friends to assist you so you're able to be the parent your child needs.

When you are understanding, and encourage, model, and facilitate the grieving process, you may be surprised at how well your child grows through grief.

My Success Strategy

I can lay some groundwork for healthy responses to mourning by teaching my child that death is a natural part of the life cycle. I equip my child with grief skills when I . . .

help your child love school

Parents, you make the difference. You can help your child become motivated about important issues like school and learning. And that motivation will last a lifetime. "The direction in which education starts a man will determine his future life," declared Plato.

Skillful parents know that education benefits not only their child individually but also the village in which children live; or as Victor Hugo recognized, "He who opens a school door, closes a prison."[1]

Regardless of your economic, racial, educational, or cultural background, when you use your powerful influence to get your child looking forward to and enjoying school, you are giving him a key to lifetime success. You're probably doing many things "right" already that help your child see the value of school. To see if you're on the right track, first try this:

Motivated for School Quiz

Give yourself five points for usually doing these, two points for occasionally, and zero points for these you never do.

_____ 1. I share happy memories or good stories of my school experiences.

_____ 2. I make positive statements about school and the opportunity to learn.

_____ 3. I go to open houses and parent/teacher meetings with an attitude of team spirit between myself and the teacher. (There are positive outcomes when parents and teachers work together.)

_____ 4. I encourage my child to listen to teachers. (Television news reporter Diane Sawyer reveals, "I think the one lesson I have learned is that there is no substitute for paying attention."[2])

_____ 5. We have school supplies purchased and identified with my child's name.

_____ 6. We follow "school" bedtimes and morning routines.

_____ 7. I model respect for teachers. (Even when you don't agree with teachers, your attitude of respect for their authority affects your child's ability to perform.)

How did you score?

Above 30 means you're doing an exceptional job of motivating your child for school and learning. Give yourself a pat on the back. A score of 20–29 is average. Remember, everyday routines and discussions send a message to your child about the importance you place on learning. Below 20 suggests there are more ways to generate enthusiasm. Your child will be an eager learner when you value education.

You've invested in your child so far; now practice these ways to build a successful academic experience right from the start.

- Establish "school" bedtimes and morning routines. A well-rested child will be less distracted and better prepared to handle the rigors of the classroom, and will learn more. Morning routines give a child security because he feels his world is organized.
- Make breakfast matter. "Consumption of this morning meal is one of the most important things a child does all day," says Erica Lesperance, a registered dietitian specially trained in pediatric nutrition. More than

thirty years of research proves "a healthy breakfast positively impacts brain function and energy level, which is extremely important for school-aged children."[3] In a 1998 Harvard/Kellogg School Breakfast Program study, kids who ate a morning meal earned higher math grades than those who skipped breakfast.[4] Whole-grain cereals such as oatmeal and bran are best for breakfast.

> Coming together is a beginning;
> Keeping together is progress;
> Working together is success.
>
> Unknown

- Go to the school's open house and parent/teacher meetings. It's during these times that you can view your child's work and school exhibits, but most important, have a say in your child's learning goals.
- Say encouraging statements to your child such as, "I'm glad you listen to your teacher," or "I'm proud you completed that homework assignment." Your statements can be prophetic.
- Get your child's hearing checked. Hearing loss is common in kids and makes it difficult for them to understand classroom instructions or learn pronunciations.
- Plan constructive use of after-school time. Children need some down time to relax after school; however, research indicates that children who watch TV more than ten hours per week are at greater risk of school failure. The humorist Groucho Marx quipped, "I find television very educational. The minute somebody turns it on, I go to the library and read a book."[5]
- Buy an inexpensive chalkboard for your child's bedroom. Write his plans, goals, or assignment for the next day and check off each when finished. The visual reminder can motivate your child to stay on task and complete more.

- Praise progress not perfection. Too many parents nitpick or nag their child for not achieving flawless schoolwork. Children get excited about improving when parents applaud small accomplishments.
- Together with your child, create thank-you notes or gifts for the teacher. *My Favorite Teachers* coupons, a $5.95 softcover book of quotes and special coupons for children to give teachers, is available at bookstores and online. You can also bake bread or cookies or make decorative soaps as a gift. One of my fond memories is when my sibling and I would gather in the kitchen with Mom to decorate soap at Christmastime. We'd cut a pretty picture from magazines and glue it onto a bar of soap Mom bought just for gift-giving. Then we'd dip it ever so gently in melted paraffin wax just to coat the picture. This made the soap useful while protecting the picture. We would package two bars of soap together in a gift box to present to our teacher. By doing this, we learned to appreciate those who taught us in the classroom. I wonder if that is why I'm an educator today.
- Decorate your child's room with a map. Maps make inexpensive wall adornments and naturally and comfortably teach geography.
- Show confidence in your child's capability in any subject. Your attitude sends a powerful and prophetic message to your child.

Remember, the teacher has your child for perhaps a year—you have your child for the full marathon of schooling. Begin now making a difference. Benjamin Franklin counseled, "An investment in knowledge always pays the best interest." Although good parenting costs time and energy, it's well worth the price.

My Success Strategy

As my child starts the first year of formal learning, I will invest in his school success by . . .

1

2

3

4

parenting anytime

a successful parent

Want to be a successful parent? We all do. Nobody's yet called my office asking how to fail at childrearing. Rather, I get calls appealing for advice, answers, or assurance. The term *successful* is subjective. What it means to your mother, or mother-in-law, might be different to you. This I know: understanding your child's needs—not just wants—and responding appropriately is one way of succeeding in raising her well. But, how do you get proficient at a job you've never done?

Right now, commit to sharpening your parenting skills, and you won't waste valuable time later. Here are essential skills for the enormous task at hand. Practicing these will help you enjoy a better relationship with your child, and you can rest in knowing you did your personal best to raise a happy, healthy contributor to society. Imagine if your little one could share her definition of success; if she could tell just how she feels, maybe she would talk like this:

I feel secure when adults run the household. *Be the parent!*

He who sharpens the ax before beginning to cut wood does not waste time.
Swahili Proverb

I feel loved when you care enough to set boundaries. *Make and keep rules.*

I get confused when you are unpredictable. *Stay dependable.*

I'm being me. *Accept my immaturity.*

I'm learning about myself. *Teach me to understand my many feelings.*

I depend on you to teach me correct ways to act. *Catch me "being good" and tell me.*

I can get embarrassed. *Correct me in private.*

I learn when I experience the results of my behavior. *Discipline with consequences.*

I'm full of questions. *Tell me answers or I'll get them elsewhere.*

I need to feel included in the family. *Assign household chores.*

I learn to trust from you. *Keep your promises.*

I need to accept my mistakes. *Admit you aren't perfect.*

I copy your ways of caring for myself. *Live a healthy lifestyle.*

I learn forgiveness and to own my behavior from you. *Apologize sometimes.*

I'll become like you even when you think I wasn't looking. *Be a good model.*

My Success Strategy

I am successful at parenting because I . . .

"am i normal?"

It may be as old as the dawn of history, but that doesn't mean childrearing is easy to do. Parenting is complex and challenging. We often feel helpless because there's no rulebook, and we wonder if we're making or breaking our kids. I wonder how my mothering compares to other moms.

There are many innovative ways to raise kids and, as I've said before, no one way is right or perfect. Years ago I stumbled across a little humor book, *Are You Normal?* by Bernice Kanner, that shared fascinating statistics about raising kids. It may be reassuring—maybe not—to see how you fare according to these stats.

Making the bed. When it comes to making the bed every morning, parents with young children usually don't. Only 19 percent of parents reported that they make this a practice although they tell their kids to do it. According to research, some dads pitch in, but only 9 percent. Just think, if your child's father makes the bed every day, he is literally one in a million.

Instead of the slogan "Got Milk?" how about "Got Magnets?" In most homes, including mine, the fridge holds more than food. About four in ten American kitchens proudly display photographs and children's artwork on the fridge along with a collection of magnets. I think that a cluttered refrigerator door is the mark of a healthy, happy family. Every once in a while I have to remove some clutter and clean off and around my fridge.

Catch the sniffles again? The "normal" child catches six to ten colds a year. Boys get sick more often than girls do. But moms succumb to colds more often than dads. I propose the reason is that Mom usually stays home with the sick kid—then she gets it.

> If at first you don't succeed, you're running about average.
> M. H. Alderson

Wash your hands? That question echoed in my home every day when Lynsey and Laura were young. American parents take pride, we have taught our children healthy hygiene practices. According to research, over half, or 54.2 percent, of our kids wash with soap and water all the time after using the restroom.

Where's your gun? Nearly two out of every five families with kids keep a firearm in the home. The unnerving part to me is that statistics say more than one in four handgun owners keep their guns loaded. Half of those handgun owners store their guns unlocked.

Hate childproof caps? Then you're normal. Those childproof medicine bottle lids aggravate one in five people—me included. I always wonder how difficult it must be for people with arthritis. The comedy of errors is that many tots figure a way to open the bottle anyhow. My sister-in-law's dog even figured it out and devoured the pills inside.

Brag on your kids? Normal again. Almost three out of four people surveyed—72 percent—admit they call their parents to boast about a child's report card. Seems we never outgrow our need for Mom or Dad's approval.

Answering the question "What's the first thing you do when you come home?" 8 percent said, "Hug my kid." Most parents reported kicking off their shoes as their first order of business. Twenty percent said they change clothes first, and 10 percent listen to the phone messages or open the mail.

Not mentioned in studies, but I'm convinced is a normal irritant, is the unsolicited sales calls that always seem to interrupt family dinner. Once, I asked the solicitor to give me his number so I could return his call when he was eating dinner. He hung up on me.

So, where do you fit? There are some areas where I'm in the majority, but I'm in the minority on others.

Today, my daughters are young adults, but I occasionally wonder if I was reasonable in my rules. Fortunately, when they were teens, Paul and I joined a class for parents of teens at our church. By talking with others about their home life and swapping stories and opinions I often drove home assured I was pretty normal. Better yet, I realized my kids were too.

My Success Strategy

Although I do the best I can, I'm normal to wonder if I'm a good enough parent. It's nice to know that I'm pretty typical because . . .

grateful, not greedy

Kids are naturally self-seeking. Our society focuses on acquisition, and while it may be more blessed to give, receiving really *is* more fun. So it's understandable why youngsters aren't grateful.

However, just because greed is to be expected, it's not to be accepted. Gratitude is a matter of learning.

As a parent, the first and most influential teacher, you must teach your impressionable tot how to be appreciative. Facing life with an attitude of gratitude will help him be more happy and content. How do you communicate this valuable message? First, slow the greed avalanche right from the start by

- Limiting TV viewing . . . especially during the holidays when advertisers target your child as a way to get into your bank account.
- Decreasing trips to toy stores. Make shopping an "adult" activity.
- Setting limits on the number of birthday and holiday "wish list" items.

- Reminding your child that his list is suggestion only. It's not a "Daddy do" list.
- Focusing on intangible wealth. Good friends, laughter, safety, and freedom are indeed welcomed gifts.

Second, you can live a grateful lifestyle. It has been said we are always teaching—sometimes we use words. Saying thank you to others or whispering grace before your meals can show gratitude. However, the most successful teaching tool is *you*. Your child is a copycat and will act like you. Smile to show appreciation to the server who hands him a glass of milk; give generous hugs to his teacher to appreciate her hard work at school; and write notes of thanks for gifts and kindness received. Your grateful behavior will teach your tyke to be grateful too. The comedian Woody Allen wrote, "I am thankful for laughter, except when milk comes out of my nose."

Notice nature. It's easy to take our environment for granted. In these early, teachable years, encourage your child to appreciate the scenery that surrounds him: the immensity of the ocean, the perfection of a snowflake, the endless night sky, or the rugged splendor of a mountain range. Marvel at the power of the wind and the stamina of a tree. I've often reminded my girls of a quote by Goethe: "Nature is the living, visible garment of God." When you are awestruck by these things, you teach your child to be fascinated by them too.

Contrast your family with those less fortunate. Remind your child that there are people in your community who aren't as blessed: families without homes and sad, lonely people without family or friends. It's never too early to show gratitude for your family.

Give to others first. When my daughters were young, one of our family traditions was to serve a meal to the homeless.

> We must . . . realize that the time is always ripe to do right.
>
> Nelson Mandela

Every Thanksgiving my husband, daughters, and I spent an evening at a rescue mission, giving away plates of hot food. After seeing hungry faces and cold, calloused hands gratefully reaching out for a free meal, my daughters heartily appreciated going home to their safe, cozy bedrooms.

I like what Webster's dictionary says of thankfulness: "impressed with a sense of kindness received." This definition takes the focus off material possessions.

As a mom, I hope my young daughters learned the art of gratitude by the way I lived and continue to live my life. I never wanted to raise children afflicted with the "gimmes." Rather, I wanted them to be women of substance. William Bennett, author of *The Moral Compass*, said, "Sometimes we need to remind ourselves that thankfulness is indeed a virtue."[1]

I believe that children who learn to be thankful early in life receive a permanent lesson in contented living.

My Success Strategy

I don't always have to use words to teach; I can use my behavior. Today I will teach my child to be grateful when I . . .

decibel dangers

Do you expect value for the price of your child's toys? What about the cost to your child's hearing when exposed to noisy toys? My parents thought it was funny to give our daughters loud musical instruments, noisemakers, and other earsplitting toys when they were young. While we were grateful for their gifts and allowed our girls to enjoy them, we used caution. The buzz, bang, and blast of noisy toys can damage a young child's hearing.

Hearing helps children distinguish speech from noise and locate the origin of a sound. During the first five years, hearing is essential to language progress, learning, obedience, higher self-confidence, and quality of life. It's a commodity to be protected. Toys emitting sounds of ninety decibels (dB) or more can cause permanent hearing loss. Toy fire trucks, ambulances, siren police cars, toy cell phones, personal stereo systems, some musical instruments, bass drums, and firecrackers fall into this deafening category. It's understandable—or scary—that the incidence of hearing loss among rock musicians is 13 to 30 percent.

Exposure to these items for brief moments will probably do no harm. We allowed our daughters to play with their loud toys but for limited amounts of time. It's repeated, long-term exposure that has potential to injure hearing. If you allow your child to play for hours in her bedroom with a screeching toy or beat on a drum set, you increase her possibility of hearing loss. If you must yell to be heard over the roar of the television, it's probably causing harm. Trust your instincts; if you have concerns that an item is too loud, it probably is. According to Bobby Alford, MD, Department of Otorhinolaryngology and Communicative Sciences, Baylor College of Medicine, 20 to 25 percent of childhood hearing impairment cases are attributable to environmental causes.[1]

> In bringing up children, spend on them half as much money and twice as much time.
>
> Author unknown

The Occupational Safety and Health Administration (OSHA) states that workplace noise or music levels over ninety dB are harmful to hearing. Though the government sets standards to protect adults, there are no federal standards to regulate acceptable noise levels on toys children play with. Many audiologists believe that any noise above eighty-five dB is potentially damaging.

So what's a parent to do? Be an advocate for your youngster. Keep her defenseless ears far from loud toys, sporting events, crowd noise, and music. Don't take her into an auditorium with deafening music and applause or put her in your backpack and mow the grass for an hour. Today, many hospitals automatically screen newborns for hearing loss. Some screen only those at high risk for loss, such as newborns with a family history of deafness or hearing problems, low birth weight, or certain other medical conditions. If your baby wasn't screened or you want another screening, ask your pediatrician. Many tots with no risk factors have hearing loss.

If you think your toddler or preschooler is not hearing well, talk to your doctor. Teach your tot to play with loud toys in larger rooms where the sound is more diluted. Also show her how to hold toys an arm's length away from her body. At least this keeps the harsh noise from being too close to her head. If necessary, remove the batteries before your tyke plays with certain toys. Limit the amount of time loud toys can be played with. Require your youngster to wear special ear protection when playing with popguns or musical instruments. Avoid giving your preschooler headsets when listening to music. Often children turn up the volume to deafening limits. If your child insists on headsets, instruct her in proper listening limits. When Lynsey and Laura were young, Laura had a tape player and Lynsey a CD boom box. With each daughter, I took time to show her the number on the volume control that represented her maximum for hearing safety . . . and my nerves. Today, it's the iPod and other portable media devices with headsets. But your teaching of safe volume limits—or setting the volume control lock—is a necessity.

Also, be aware that environmental noise can emit a dangerous 90 dB or more. Items around your home include lawn mowers (107 dB), power tools (110 dB), the average iPod on 5/10 setting (94 dB), or even loud piano music (92–95 dB). Again, short bursts of these sounds probably do no harm; it's regular, sustained exposure that causes permanent damage. There are free publications on hearing from the National Institute on Deafness and Other Communication Disorders at www.nidcd.nih.gov.

Hearing loss can be attributed to genetic susceptibility or certain illnesses, but we can try to prevent loss by using caution when purchasing or playing with noisemakers.

My Success Strategy

The earlier I know about hearing loss, the sooner I can protect my child's hearing. One thing I can do today is . . .

prudent parenting

When Lynsey and Laura were young, Paul and I were as poor as skinny church mice. If you can identify, then you'll appreciate these smart ways to stretch your household budget. As you give time and attention to saving money, be sure to involve your tot. These "recipes" teach your tot to reuse, plus you'll stimulate his overall development in the process.

Recycled Crayons

Rather than buying new crayons, gather:

1 old muffin tin (or a silicone muffin pan)
Broken crayon pieces
Nonstick cooking spray

Generously spray nonstick cooking spray into a muffin tin. Instruct your tot to tear off any remaining paper from the crayon pieces. Scatter the pieces into each muffin cup. Different colors can be mixed in the same cup. Bake at 275° for ten to twenty minutes. Remove from the oven and cool.

Use a knife to dislodge the crayon "blocks" from each muffin cup. Your "new" crayons can be used as-is or broken into smaller tot-sized pieces for easier handling.

Now get out the paper and enjoy a colorful experience. With the different pieces melted together, each stroke of the new crayon reveals a rainbow of color. This activity supports your child's small motor, language, emotional, and social skills while strengthening his eye-hand coordination—a precursor to reading and writing abilities.

> Foraging gives us the ability to view the old and abandoned in a new light—reclaiming them from oblivion with creativity and choice.
>
> Sarah Ban Breathnach

Homemade Diaper Wipes

A homemade alternative to commercial wet wipes is this recipe.

1 roll paper towels
3 cups water
1 tablespoon baby shampoo
1 tablespoon baby oil
1 airtight container (old wet-wipe box)

Cut the roll of towels in half with a sharp knife. Remove and discard the inner cardboard tube. Place half roll of towels into a container. Involve your child by inviting him to slowly stir the water, shampoo, and oil in a large bowl. Stirring is excellent for small motor skills, hand and wrist flexibility. Then carefully pour this mix over the half roll in the container. Tell your tot to snap the box closed. After about twenty-four hours, the paper towels will soak up the mild cleansing mix. When you need to wipe a sweet face or dirty bottom, simply pull a moist, fresh-smelling, and economical sheet from the middle of the roll.

Anytime you use fractions and counting to bake or create something with your child, you are increasing his math skills. Children absorb information better when they're having fun.

To stretch your toy budget, read Malissa Copeland's "Homemade Toddler Toys" article in *The Dollar Stretcher* magazine, www.stretcher.com/stories/00/000821i.cfm. For preschoolers and kindergartners, print out these games at www.first-school.ws/theme/hometoys.htm.

My Success Strategy

Homemade alternatives can save me time, money, and gas. A new homemade idea I'm going to try is . . .

show your love all year

A tender reminder of showing affection toward those we love is on Valentine's Day in February. Most parents use this occasion to express love to their youngsters. The temptation to always use toys or gifts as a symbol of love is strong. But there are a multitude of no-cost ways to communicate your powerful message every day. Saying "I love you" is good, but showing "I love you" is better. Use this chapter to help you show affection all year long. Although the suggestions seem simple, they are profoundly effective because children who feel loved act differently from those who feel unloved. If your child is:

Zero to six months—nestle her in your arms and hold the bottle when feeding her (no impersonal bottle propping); look in a mirror together and repeat her name aloud; immediately respond to her cries; lovingly gaze into her eyes; read picture books to her; place her on the floor several times daily to allow her room to exercise muscles.

Six to twelve months—teach her the name of her body parts; although messy, permit her to hold a spoon/cup at mealtimes; expect her to grab, taste, touch, poke, pour, and dump everything; safety proof; use positive discipline such as redirection; sing songs and play peekaboo together; keep regular bath/bedtimes; and read storybooks aloud to her.

> The supreme happiness in life is the conviction that we are loved.
>
> Victor Hugo

Twelve to twenty-four months—display her scribbles/artwork on your refrigerator; allow some separation, negativism, and independent behavior; encourage genuine affection—never force or coerce a child to hug someone else; when possible offer two simple choices; include your toddler in small chores like sorting laundry or wiping up spills; read storybooks together; discipline with immediate and related consequences and be consistent in your expectations, responses, and words.

Three to five years—appreciate your preschooler's need to separate and want independence; understand—but don't overlook—bossiness as part of language and social development; encourage self-help skills like dressing without your help, teeth brushing, and washing/drying her own hands; teach independent living tasks like how to prepare her cereal or toast, then give positive feedback for effort; be consistent in your discipline; allow free time just to play, don't overschedule the life of your child; let her read aloud to you; be available but not intrusive when she's playing contently; ask open-ended questions to encourage heartfelt conversation; be patient and avoid saying, "Hurry up!"

You are the major influence in your child's sense of worth. Children who feel valued by their parents become happier, healthier, and more productive adults. Today and every day, affirm your child, discipline, nurture, and watch for progress, not perfection.

My Success Strategy

Showing love means trying to understand my child's development and to appropriately respond. I will love by doing . . .

conclusion

Children are complex and unique beings, yet they do have much in common. From the moment they come into our lives they bring us exhilaration and exhaustion. And raising children is the greatest—most challenging—career any person can attempt. But the profits are beyond compare. Among your trials and triumphs, delights and disasters, mundane and miraculous, know that much of what your child does is normal.

I once saw a bumper sticker that said, "Childhood is a journey, not a race." Are you prepared to be your child's journey *mate*? Rise above your doubts, fears, or busy schedule and *walk* through each day in this short season in your life.

appendix a: gift-giving ideas

Anxious over the right gift for your youngster? Or is your child bringing home party invitations from kids you don't even know? If you feel yourself saying "good grief!" rather than "good gift," maybe these age-appropriate ideas will help.

Three rules apply to a child's gift:

- Safety. Look for well-made, nontoxic toys and follow the manufacturer's safety information. You can also read *Consumer Reports* magazine and be alert to product recalls.
- Multiple senses. Ideally your gift should stimulate as many of the senses as possible: sight, smell, touch, taste, and hearing. The more senses involved, the longer a toy's play value.
- Age appropriateness. Avoid giving items that are too simple or too complicated. Sometimes people invest in toys for tots that are so simple the child loses interest. Frequently adults give items that are meant for older kids. The thought is they'll grow into the toy. But what usually happens is the item is put away and

often forgotten. Read and follow the manufacturer's age recommendation on toys, books, and games. If you're buying for your own child, watch what toys he plays with or what attracts attention. If you're looking for someone else's child, ask the parents what interests their child.

Here are some general ideas according to age:

Age	Gift Idea
Newborn	Attention: the best "gift" for a newborn is attention.
	Savings bond/educational IRAs: long-lasting gifts that parents appreciate
	Infant seat
2–6 months	Mobile, crib gym
	Activity center
	Balls of all sizes
	Lightweight rattle
	Blocks
	Table-top batting toys
	Bath time floating toys: sponges, boats, ducks
	Lullaby books/music
	Classical music: stimulates brain development
	Vinyl or cloth books with large pictures
	Colorful teething rings
	Blankets with textures and brightly colored surfaces
6–12 months	Cause/effect toys
	Mirrors
	Balls of all sizes
	Bath toys: items that splash or pour water
	Cloth or cardboard books with large pictures
	Soft blocks

Age	Gift Idea
	Teething toys
	Soft stuffed animals or dolls
	Finger foods
	Infant tableware
1–2 years	Cardboard books with simple pictures
	Push/pull toys
	Child-sized furniture
	Pounding and banging toys
	Stacking/nesting cups
	Grocery cart with plastic foods
	Shape sorter
	Basic 3–5 piece puzzles
	Safety gate for stairs
2 years	Paper-paged books including a Toddlers Bible
	Musical instruments
	Fat crayons/markers/pencils and paper
	Potty chair or insert
	Wagon and other riding toys
	Construction toys
	Dolls
	Kids kitchen equipment, toy telephone
	Farm animal set
	Climbing toys
	Tricycle and helmet
	Large 4–5 piece puzzles
	Sidewalk chalk
3 years	Costumes, dress-up clothing
	Dolls, teddy bears
	Toy telephone, lawnmower, vacuum, cars, trucks

Age	Gift Idea
	Slides, swings, balancing beams
	Stickers
	Wagon
	Playdough and clay
	Trampoline
	Puzzles
	Shape/color educational materials
	Board/card games
	Scissors and nontoxic art supplies with supervision
4 years	Low-maintenance pet
	Pretend toys, play money, telephone
	Jungle gym
	Stringing beads
	Lacing cards
	Paper-paged books
	Tape recorder, audio tapes, sing-along tapes and videos
	Musical instruments
	Dolls
	Clay
	Bicycle and helmet
	Roller skates and helmet
	Board/card games
5 years	Sports equipment, jump ropes
	Stationery and postage stamps
	Craft kits
	Construction toys
	Books including an encyclopedia set
	Modeling clay
	Bicycle and helmet

Age	Gift Idea
	Board/card/video games
	Camera
	Stamping kit
	Child-sized sleeping bag
	Coloring books, crayons, markers
	Walkie-talkie

I feel the best toys don't have cords, batteries, or microchips. Instead, they rely on a youngster's natural resource—imagination. Ever watch a kid play with an empty box?

A unique gift is that of experience. Enroll a preschooler in a class at your local recreation center so he learns a new skill. Offer to take a child on your family vacation or pay his way to camp. Experiences give rich and lasting memories. And there's no price tag on those valuable gifts.

appendix b: zero to five child development guide

We talked in the mall's bathroom (women do that—my husband thinks it's weird) while she wrangled her kids. I told her I was writing this book. "Oh!" she begged. "Please make a chapter on normal development in the early years. Sometimes I just want to know if what my kids do is normal."

In response to this mother of two toddlers, and because I hear a similar concern from audiences everywhere, here are some guides in early childhood development.

In the first five years there are four domains of development to observe: language, motor, social, and cognitive (intellectual). Language includes hearing and understanding words (auditory comprehension) and the reproduction of them (verbal ability).

Motor skills, particularly, develop from the spine outward. So the large trunk muscles are mastered first, usually in the first year of life. Then the small, or fine, motor skills, like use of the fingers, develop last.

Social development is rooted in the desire for human interaction. That's why you'll see an infant looking intently at Mom and Dad or studying the person holding him.

Cognitive or intellectual development begins at birth; one of the earliest visible signs is when an infant maneuvers his fist into his mouth and sucks on it.

To watch each domain unfold from its fundamental beginning into a battery of refined skills is a rare privilege. As you read this, I hope you'll be assured of your child's developmental progress as well as what to expect in coming months.

Age	Guide
0–12 months	Develops attachment/trust in primary caregiver
	Gains head and limb control
	Puts everything into mouth
	Reaches out to grasp/transfer objects
	Rolls from side to side
	Goes from sitting up to crawling to cruising
	Listens to sounds
	Babbles to saying "ma ma" or "da da"
	Follows objects with the eyes (tracks)
	Can sleep twelve to eighteen hours a day
	Expresses fear of being abandoned
	Begins to laugh/show pleasure
1–2 years	Walks/explores surroundings
	Driven by curiosity
	Fearless
	Grabs and gets into everything
	Usually takes one long nap each day
	Content to play alone (parent is the best friend)
	Thrives on routines
	Examines own body/points to body parts
	Does not understand how to—nor want to—share

Age	Guide
	Very alert and active with a short attention span
	Eats variety of table foods/drinks from a cup
	Says first whole words to saying simple sentences
	Begins to ask many questions
	Runs stiffly at first
	Climbs/pulls/pushes
	Copies adult behaviors/words
	Egocentric
2–3 years	Quadrupled birth weight
	Thrives on routines
	Scribbles
	Understands more words than can say
	Is negative: "No!"
	Egocentric: "Mine!"
	Uses short sentences
	Copies adult behaviors/mimics words
	Wants relationship with parents
	Feeds self
	Energetic
	Removes own clothing
	Insists on own way
	Runs/climbs/hops/jumps/dances to music
	Parallel play (alongside peers but not with them)
	Learning—but limited ability—to share
	Usually toilet trained
3 years	Decreased appetite/food wars/food favorites
	Masters large motor skills
	Developing fine motor skills; hands may have tremors
	Colors/cuts with scissors/zips

Age	Guide
	Performs self-help tasks; feeds/undresses/dresses self
	May not sleep at nap time
	Bedtime resistance results in battles
	Imagination soars with pretend friends/monsters/nightmares
	Can make own voice loud/soft
	Uses about nine hundred words
	Sassy/argumentative/talkative
	Attaches to parent of opposite sex
	Shows annoyance with parents/peers
	Peer conscious/developing first real friendships
	Can wait for turn/play board and card games
	Stuttering is common; 90 percent of kids outgrow it within a few months
	Usually toilet trained
	Distinguishes boys from girls (gender aware)
	Releases anxiety by thumb-sucking/nail-biting
4 years	Adventurous
	Needs eleven hours sleep in a twenty-four-hour cycle
	Dawdles/stalls
	Active imagination/will exaggerate
	Speech is clear and understandable
	"Why," "hate," and "please" frequently used
	Bossy/boastful
	Performs self-help tasks; brushes teeth/washes and dries hands/combs hair/makes bed
	Names colors/shapes/numbers/seasons
5 years	Follows two-step directions
	Establishes right or left handedness
	Needs eleven hours sleep in a twenty-four-hour cycle
	Plays in groups/wants to be boss

Age	Guide
	Imagined power over people/events
	Sensitive to ridicule/perfectionist/fear of failure
	Silliness/"potty" talk
	May appear less active due to longer attention span
	Recognizes size proportion: "She got more!"
	Interest in collecting and organizing/lines things in a row

appendix c: deeper reading resource list

Additional resources can empower you in these foundation years of parenting. This index is a sampling of the buffet of resources you can find at your favorite bookstore or public library. Please take advantage of this list.

Biting

No Biting, Horrible Crocodile! Jonathan Shipton (New York: Golden Books, 1995).

No Biting! Karen Katz (New York: Grosset & Dunlap, 2002).

Teeth Are Not for Biting. Elizabeth Verdick (Minneapolis: Free Spirit Publishing, 2003).

Brain Research

Building Healthy Minds: The Six Experiences That Create Intelligence and Emotional Growth in Babies and Young

Children. Stanley Greenspan, MD (Cambridge, MA: Perseus Books, 2000).

The Power of Mother Love: Strengthening the Bond between You and Your Child. Brenda Hunter, PhD (Colorado Springs, CO: Waterbrook Press, 1999).

Smart Baby, Clever Child: Brain-Building Games, Activities, and Ideas to Stimulate Your Baby's Mind. Valentine Dmitriev (Avon, MA: Adams Media Corporation, 2003).

Cabin Fever

The Early Childhood Almanac: Activities for Every Month of the Year. Dana Newmann (New York: The Center for Applied Research in Education, 1997).

The Wiggle & Giggle Busy Book: 365 Fun, Physical Activities for Your Toddler and Preschooler. Trish Kuffner (Minnetonka, MN: Meadowbrook, 2005).

Children's Fears

Extreme Fear, Shyness, and Social Phobia. Louis A. Schmidt and Jay Schulkin (New York: Oxford University Press, 1999).

Go Away, Big Green Monster. Ed Emberley (Boston: L,B Kids, 1993).

Discipline

Helping Your Kids Make Good Choices. Kendra Smiley (Ann Arbor: Vine Books, 2000).

How to Behave So Your Children Will, Too! Sal Severe, PhD (New York: Viking, 2000).

Positive Discipline for Preschoolers: For Their Early Years. Jane Nelsen, EdD, Cheryl Erwin, and Roslyn Ann Duffy (New York: Three Rivers Press, 2007).

Spare the Child. Philip Greven (New York: Vintage Books, 1992).

Early Childhood Development

Caring for Your Baby and Young Child: Birth to Age 5. American Academy of Pediatrics (New York: Bantam Books, 2004).

The First Three Years of Life, revised edition. Burton L. White, PhD (New York: Fireside, 1995).

Is This "Just a Phase?" Susan Anderson Swedo, MD, and Henrietta L. Leonard, MD (New York: Broadway, 1999).

Right from Birth: Building Your Child's Foundation for Life—Birth to 18 Months. Craig T. Ramey, PhD, and Susan L. Ramey, PhD (New York: Goddard Press, 1999).

Touchpoints, Your Child's Emotional and Behavioral Development. T. Berry Brazelton, MD (Reading, MA: Da Capo Lifelong Books, 1992).

What to Expect: The First Year. A. Eisenberg, H. E. Murkoff, and S. E. Hathaway, B.S.N. (New York: Simon & Schuster, 2004).

What to Expect: The Toddler Years. A. Eisenberg, H. E. Murkoff, and S. E. Hathaway, B.S.N. (New York: Simon & Schuster, 1996).

Eating

Feeding Your Child for Lifelong Health: Birth through Age 6. Susan B. Roberts, PhD, and Melvil B. Heyman, MD (New York: Bantam Books, 1999).

First Meals. Annabel Karmel (New York: DK Adult, 2004).

One Bite Won't Kill You: More Than 200 Recipes to Tempt Even the Pickiest Eater. Ann Hodgeman (Boston: Houghton-Mifflin Co., 1999).

Fatherhood

In the Beginning, There Were No Diapers: Laughing and Learning in the First Years of Fatherhood. Tim Bete (Notre Dame, IN: Sorin Books, 2005).

The Daddy Guide: Real Life Advice and Tips from Over 250 Dads and Other Experts. Kevin Nelson (New York: McGraw-Hill, 1998).

The Joy of Fatherhood: The First Twelve Months. Marcus Jacob Goldman, MD (New York: Three Rivers Press, 2000).

The Modern Dad's Handbook. John Badalament (Cole Valley Mill, 2007).

Rattled: Surviving Your Baby's First Year Without Losing Your Cool. Trish Berg (Portland: Multnomah, 2008).

Wisdom of Our Fathers: Lessons and Letters from Daughters and Sons. Tim Russert (New York: Random House, 2007).

Grief

The Mourning Handbook: The Most Complete Resource Offering Practical and Compassionate Advice on Coping with All Aspects of Death and Dying. Helen Fitzgerald (New York: Simon & Schuster, 1995).

When Dinosaurs Die: A Guide to Understanding Death. Laurene Kasny Brown (Boston: Little, Brown Young Readers, 1998).

Kindergarten Readiness

Choosing a School for Your Child. Item #328R (Consumer Information Catalog, 2004).

Kindergarten, Ready or Not? A Parents Guide. Sean A. Walmsley and Bonnie Brown (Portsmouth: Heinemann, 1996).

The Kissing Hand. Audrey Penn (Terre Haute, IN: Tanglewood Press, 2006).

Tom Goes to Kindergarten. Margaret Wild (Morton Grove, IL: Albert Whitman & Company, 2000).

What Your Kindergartner Needs to Know. E.D. Hirsch Jr. (New York: Delta, 1997).

Play

The House of Make-Believe: Children's Play and the Developing Imagination. D.G. Singer and J.L. Singer (Cambridge, MA: Harvard University Press, 1990).

The Power of Parent-Child Play. Laurie Winslow Sargent (Enumclaw, WA: WinePress, 2005).

Reading Aloud

Raising Readers: Helping Your Child to Literacy. Steven Bialostok (Winnipeg: Peguis, 1992).

Reading with Babies, Toddlers and Twos. Susan Straub and KJ Dell'Antonia (Naperville, IL: Sourcebooks, 2006).

Safety

Baby Proofing Basics: How to Keep Your Child Safe, 2nd edition. Vicki Lansky (Minnetonka, MN: Book Peddlers, 2002).

The Safe Baby: A Do-It-Yourself Guide for Home Safety. Debra Smiley Holtzman (Boulder, CO: Sentient Publications, 2004).

School Success

The ABCs of School Success. Wesley Sharpe, EdD (Grand Rapids: Revell, 2008).

You Know Your Child Is Gifted When . . . A Beginner's Guide to Life on the Bright Side. Judy Galbraith (Minneapolis: Free Spirit, 2000).

Self-Esteem

The Five Love Languages of Children. Gary Chapman and Ross Campbell, MD (Chicago: Moody Press, 1997).

How to Really Love Your Child, rev. edition. Ross D. Campbell, MD (Wheaton, IL: Victor Books, 1992).

Me, Myself and I: How Children Build Their Sense of Self. Kyle D. Pruett, MD (New York: Goddard Press, 1999).

Sleep Issues

Food Fights and Bedtime Battles: A Working Parent's Guide to Negotiating. Tim Jordan (New York: Berkley Trade, 2001).

The No-Cry Sleep Solution: Gentle Ways to Help Your Baby Sleep Through the Night. Elizabeth Pantley and William Sears (Chicago: McGraw-Hill, 2002).

The Sleep Book for Tired Parents: Help for Solving Children's Sleep Problems. Rebecca Hundley (Seattle: Parenting Press, Inc., 1991).

Solve Your Child's Sleep Problems. Richard Ferber, MD (New York: Fireside, 2006).

Winning Bedtime Battles: How to Help Your Child Develop Good Sleep Habits. C.E. Schaefer, PhD, and T.F. DiGeronimo, MED (New York: Citadel Press, 1992).

Stress

KidStress: What It Is—How It Feels—How to Help. George Witkin, PhD (New York: Penguin, 2000).

Rattled: Surviving Your Baby's First Year Without Losing Your Cool. Trish Berg (Portland: Multnomah, 2008).

Stress and Your Child: Stress in Children and Prevention Strategies. Archibald Hart, PhD (Nashville: Thomas Nelson, 2005).

Tantrums

Tantrums: Secrets to Calming the Storm. Ann E. La Forge (New York: Pocketbooks, 1996).

Trouble in Paradise: Temper Tantrums. VHS video (Wheeling, IL: Film Ideas, Inc., 1996).

Thumbsucking

Helping the Thumb-Sucking Child. Rosemary A. Van Norman (Garden City, NY: Avery Publishing Group, 1999).

How to Stop Thumbsucking (and Other Oral Habits): Practical Solutions for Home and Therapy. Pam Marshalla (Kirkland, WA: Marshalla Speech and Language, 2001).

Toilet Teaching

Everyone Poops. Taro Gomi (Brooklyn, NY: Kane/Miller Book Publishers, 2001).

Once Upon a Potty for Her. Alona Frankel (Buffalo, NY: Firefly, 2007).

Once Upon a Potty for Him. Alona Frankel (Buffalo, NY: Firefly, 2007).

The No-Cry Potty Training Solution: Gentle Ways to Help Your Child Say Good-Bye to Diapers. Elizabeth Pantley (New York: McGraw-Hill, 2006).

Online Resources

Breast-feeding: *www.breastfeeding.com*

Brenda Nixon, speaker: parent tips, books, and more *www.BrendaNixon.com*

Federal Citizen Information Center: free or low-cost family booklets *www.pueblo.gsa.gov*

Home Safety Advantage: tips and products to baby proof *www.babyhomesafety.com*

Kids In Danger: children's product safety, recalls *www.kidsindanger.org*

National Fatherhood Initiative: helping you become a better dad *www.fatherhood.org*

Parenting Resources from Jean Tracy: *www.kidsdiscuss.com*

Parenting: articles from Focus on the Family *www.family.org/parenting/*

Parents As Teachers: child development, brain research *www.patnc.org*

The I'm Safe! Network: product recalls, child safety articles *www.imsafe.com*

The Parent Institute: information, links to parenting sites *www.parent-institute.com*

U.S. Consumer Product Safety Commission: product safety *www.cpsc.gov*

Zero to Three: resources for parents on the first years of life *www.zerotothree.org*

notes

The Right Start

1. Trish Berg, *Rattled: Surviving Your Baby's First Year Without Losing Your Cool* (Colorado Springs: Multnomah, 2008), 172.
2. Ibid., 154.

"Is She Normal?"

1. "Baby Spit-Up: What's Normal, What's Not," Parenthood.com, http://www.parenthood.com/articles.html?article_id=2361 (accessed January 2008).

The Wonders of Mother's Milk

1. "Position of the American Dietetic Association: Promoting and Supporting Breastfeeding," *J Am Diet Assoc.* 1005 (May 2005): 810–18.
2. L. John Horwood and David M. Fergusson, "Breastfeeding and Later Cognitive and Academic Outcomes," *Pediatrics* 101 no. 1 (January 1998): 9.
3. William C. Heird, "Progress in Promoting Breast-feeding, Combating Malnutrition, and Composition and Use of Infant Formula, 1981–2006," *The Journal of Nutrition* 137 (2007): 499S-502S.

Grow a Reader

1. Wesley Sharpe, *The ABCs of School Success* (Grand Rapids: Revell, 2008).
2. Ibid.

Quality Childcare Checklist

1. "Trends in Labor Force Participation of Married Mothers of Infants," *Monthly Labor Review*, February 2007, http://www.bls.gov/opub/mlr/2007/02/art2full.pdf (accessed January 2008).

2. "Not for the Money," *Psychology Today*, May 1992, http://psychologytoday.com/articles/pto-19920501-000018.html (accessed January 2008).

3. Berg, *Rattled*, 3.

Starting Solid Foods

1. "Introducing Solid Foods: What You Need to Know," MayoClinic.com, June 2006, http://www.mayoclinic.com/health/healthy-baby/PR00029 (accessed January 2008).

2. "Starting Solids by Dr Jack Newman MD, FRCPC," Express Yourself Mums, http://www.expressyourselfmums.co.uk/article.asp?case_id=56 (accessed January 2008).

3. Ibid.

Protect Those Peepers

1. "This Summer Keep an Eye on UV Safety," American Academy of Ophthalmology, http://www.aao.org/newsroom/release/20070629.cfm (accessed December 2007).

2. "Skin Cancer Prevention and Early Detection," http://www.cancer.org/docroot/PED/content/ped_7_1_Skin_Cancer_Detection_What_You_Can_Do.asp (accessed December 2007).

3. "Protecting Kids from the Sun," http://www.ftc.gov/bcp/edu/pubs/consumer/health/hea13.shtm (accessed December 2007).

Ten Tips for Stress-*less* Parenting

1. "The Stress of Parenting," *Canadian Mental Health Association*, http://www.cmha.ca/bins/content_page.asp?cid=2-70-71 (accessed December 2007).

2. Craig H. Hart, "What Children Need from Parents," *Marriage & Families*, Spring 2004, http://marriageandfamilies.byu.edu/issues/2004/Spring/childrensneed.aspx (accessed December 2007).

Father Facts

1. Hart, "What Children Need from Parents."

2. http://www.quotedb.com/quotes/1188 (accessed June 2008).

Break the Bottle Habit

1. "Children's Health Topics: Oral Health," *American Academy of Pediatrics*, http://www.aap.org/healthtopics/oralhealth.cfm (accessed January 2008).

A Toilet Teaching Hurdle

1. Bruce Taubman, "Toilet Training and Toileting Refusal for Stool Only: A Prospective Study," *Pediatrics* 99, no. 1 (January 1997): 54–58, http://pediatrics.aappublications.org/cgi/content/abstract/99/1/54 (accessed January 2008).

To Spank or Not?

1. Burton L. White, PhD, *The First Three Years of Life*, new and revised edition (New York: Fireside, 1993), 253.
2. Ibid.
3. Nancy Samalin and Catherine Whitney, "What's Wrong with Spanking?" *Parents* 70, no. 5 (May 1995): 35–36.
4. Murray A. Straus, PhD, David B. Sugarman, PhD, and Jean Giles-Sims, PhD, "Spanking by Parents and Subsequent Antisocial Behavior of Children," Arch Pediatr Adolesc Med/Vol. 151, August 1997.
5. Ibid.

Clinging Toddlers

1. Brenda Hunter, PhD, *What Every Mother Needs to Know* (Sisters: Multnomah, 1993), 162.

The Power of Play

1. Dorothy Singer and Jerome Singer, *The House of Make Believe* (Cambridge: Harvard University Press, 1990), 64.
2. "What They Say about Play," http://www.scribd.com/doc/22929/play-quotes (accessed June 2008).

Choosing the Right Preschool

1. Grace Ketterman, *Mothering: The Complete Guide for Mothers of All Ages* (Colorado Springs: Chariot Victor Publications, 1994).

Raise Responsible Kids

1. http://www.tv.com/ray-romano/person/1561/summary.html (accessed February 2008).
2. Deborah McClellan, MS, "Raising Responsible Kids," *Parenting 24/7,* June 2005, http://www.parenting247.org/article.cfm?ContentID=604&challenge=8&AgeGroup=2 (accessed December 2007).
3. http://thinkexist.com/quotation/children_have_never_been_very_good_at_listening/147956.html.

What Children Really Need

1. Elaine M. Gibson, "Kids Demand Attention . . . Naturally," n.d., http://elainegibson.net/parenting/attention.html (accessed January 2008).
2. Ibid.
3. http://www.vivamiracle.com/qdb/select.php?action=2&autor=all (accessed March 2008).
4. Philip E. Veerman, *The Rights of the Child and the Changing Image of Childhood* (Martinus Nijhoff Publishers, 1992), 248–49.

5. David N. Elkins, "Spirituality," *Psychology Today*, Sept/Oct 1999, www.psychologytoday.com/articles/pro-19990901-000036.html (accessed January 2008).

6. Emerson Roy West, *Vital Quotations* (Salt Lake City: Bookcraft, 1968), 118.

7. http://www.brainyquote.com/quotes/authors/n/nelson_mandela.html (accessed March 2008).

Thumb-Sucking Sally

1. http://www.drgreene.org/body.cfm?xyzpdqabc=0&id=21&action=detail&ref=856 (accessed January 2008).

Bedtime Resistance Remedy

1. Richard Ferber, MD, *Solve Your Child's Sleep Problems* (New York: Fireside, 1985).

Help Your Child Love School

1. www.worldofquotes.com/author/Victor-Hugo/1/index.html (accessed March 2008).

2. www.brainyquote.com/quotes/authors/d/diane_sawyer.html (accessed March 2008).

3. http://www.thedietchannel.com/5-Important-Reasons-Your-Child-Should-Eat-Breakfast.htm, The Diet Channel (accessed December 2007).

4. J. Michael Murphy, EdD, "Universal-Free School Breakfast Program Evaluation Design Project," *USDA, Food and Nutrition Service*, December 22, 1999, www.fns.usda.gov/oane/menu/DemoProjects/sbppilot/SBPlitreview.PDF (accessed December 2007).

5. www.watchfuleye.com/groucho.html (accessed March 2008).

Grateful, Not Greedy

1. William J. Bennett, *The Moral Compass: Stories for a Life's Journey* (New York: Simon & Schuster, 1995).

Decibel Dangers

1. Baylor College of Medicine, http://www.bcm.edu.oto/grand/31193.html (accessed June 2008).

Born in Ohio, **Brenda Nixon** (www.BrendaNixon.com) lived in Missouri and Idaho before returning to her home state, where she and her husband, Paul, live with miniature dachshund Opie. Brenda is the mother of two daughters, Lynsey and Laura.

Brenda earned a master's degree in religious education from Nazarene Theological Seminary and worked as a preschool teacher, nanny, psychiatric chaplain, an educational toy consultant, and a certified parent educator for the Kansas City, Missouri, school district. During her years in Kansas City, she was the parenting expert for Fox TV4 Noon News.

Today, Brenda speaks across the country to parents and professionals who serve children. She is the author of *Parenting Power in the Early Years,* co-author of *A Scrapbook of Christmas Firsts,* and contributing author to twenty-four books. Her articles appear in numerous regional and national parenting publications, she is quoted in *Woman's Day,* WebMD, *USA Today,* and MOPS International, and she's a frequent media guest sharing childrearing tips and encouragement.

Nixon, Brenda.

The birth to five
book

